NEW YORK
Real Estate Exam Review

THIRD EDITION

Eileen Taus,
Consulting Editor

Dearborn™
Real Estate Education

President: Roy Lipner
Publisher: Evan Butterfield
Managing Editor, Print Products: Louise Benzer
Development Editor: Christopher Oler
Production Coordinator: Dan Frey
Typesetter: Janet Schroeder

© 1997, 2000, 2004 by Dearborn Financial Publishing, Inc.®

Published by Dearborn™ Real Estate Education,
a division of Dearborn Financial Publishing, Inc.®
30 South Wacker Drive
Chicago, Illinois 60606-1719
(312) 836-4400
www.dearbornRE.com

Printed in the United States of America.

04 05 06 10 9 8 7 6 5 4 3

CONTENTS

■ Broker's Syllabus Topic

■ Salesperson's Syllabus Topic

INTRODUCTION & INSTRUCTION

Most new licensees describe preparing for their real estate exam as a challenging, rewarding and traumatic experience, all at the same time. For some, mastering the complex rules and special jargon of the real estate industry can be as demanding as learning a foreign language. Students who have not attended classes or studied for exams for several years sometimes find it difficult to get back into the habit—particularly when they have other important demands on their time, and homework is just another responsibility among many.

Dearborn™ Real Estate Education is aware of the particular challenges that face today's real estate students in preparing for the New York real estate licensing examinations. The *New York Real Estate Exam Review* was written with your needs in mind.

This review is designed to be used in close conjunction with *Modern Real Estate Practice in New York,* 8th Edition, by Edith Lank. Each chapter in the review corresponds to a chapter in the main text. That makes it easy for you to review specific issues that may still be difficult. The review is designed to simultaneously reinforce your comprehension of important points and identify those areas that may need additional study.

This book will help you organize and focus your exam preparations. It is NOT intended to replace classroom attendance, assigned classwork, or thorough study of your textbook and class notes!

No one ever passed a test by not studying. Similarly, it's the rare licensee who started a successful professional career by staying up all night with a pot of coffee, cramming for the next day's exam. It takes time, work, and organization to ensure the result you want.

After finishing this book, you should be able to:

- define and explain fundamental concepts and vocabulary of the real estate industry;
- identify and understand the characteristics of various legal and financial relationships involved in a real estate transaction; and
- apply your basic comprehension in an exam-style situation.

By working through the various components of each chapter, you will be sharpening your test-taking skills (key to passing the exam), as well as reinforcing your understanding of the real estate industry (key to a successful career).

■ HOW TO USE THIS BOOK

Topic Review

This question-and-answer style summary covers the most important points from the corresponding chapter of *Modern Real Estate Practice in New York*, 8th Edition. You can just read through the material for a quick review or test yourself by covering the bullet-point answers to each question with a slip of paper. Can you answer the question, including all the information contained in each point? If not, you should review the main text until you can!

Key Terms Glossary

One of the most demanding things about the real estate exam is vocabulary. If you don't know what the words mean, it's very hard to answer the question. Review these Key Terms and their definitions until they're part of your everyday language.

Pass-Point Checklist

This checklist includes the basic topics you need to master to ensure success on the exam. As you go through the list, check off those items you already know. Then go back to *Modern Real Estate Practice in New York* and your class notes and review the rest. Keep repeating those steps until you can check off every item.

Practice Questions

Each chapter includes ten exam-style multiple-choice questions that review just the material covered in the first two sections of the Review chapter. The Review also includes four full-length practice licensing exams—two 50 question exams for salespersons and two 100 question exams for brokers.

■ Note: all the practice exams include material from the main textbook that may not be included in this review!
■ Broker's license candidates: Note that you are responsible for knowing both the broker' and salesperson's material. It's a good idea for you to take the salesperson's practice exam, too!

Answer Key

After each Practice Questions section you may go to the complete set of answers (and brief explanations) included in the Answer Key for Chapters 1 through 26 found on page 137. The Practice Exam answer keys include chapter references to *Modern Real Estate Practice in New York*, 8th Edition.

You'll also find an Appendix, called Preparing for the Real Estate License Exam. It's filled with exam-taking tips and strategies to help ensure your success.

Measure Your Success

Keep track of which topics you've mastered (and which ones need more study) by recording your score for each chapter's multiple-choice exam. Remember, a score of 70% or higher is required to pass the New York licensing exam.

Good luck on the licensing exam, and best wishes for your new career.

1

LICENSE LAW

■ TOPIC REVIEW

What are the basic requirements for a real estate salesperson license?

- Complete a 45-hour approved course
- Be at least 18 years old
- Be sponsored by a licensed broker

What are the requirements for a real estate broker's license?

- Complete an additional 45 hours of approved study
- Be at least 19 years old
- Have one full year of experience as a licensed salesperson or two full years in related experience

Are there any other requirements for New York real estate licensees?

- All New York real estate licensees must be permanent U.S. residents.
- No licensee may have been convicted of a felony.
- Both salespersons and brokers must pass a state examination.
- The license period is two years; a broker's license costs $150; a salesperson's is $50.

Are there other license options or exemptions?

- A qualified broker may elect to continue working as a salesperson by obtaining an associate broker license and designating a licensed, supervising broker.
- Attorneys licensed to practice in New York are exempt from the real estate license law's licensure provisions (unless they employ real estate salespersons), and do not have to take the licensing examination.
- The following are also exempt: public officials who are performing official public duties; persons who engage in real estate activities under a court order; and resident managers who collect rent and manage property on behalf of a single owner. Some New York City tenant organizations and not-for-profit corporations are also exempt. The Broker associate is one who has all the qualifications of a Broker but elects to maintain the status of a salesperson.

Who administers the license law in New York?

- The license laws governing the real estate profession, as well as the rules and regulations that implement those laws, are administered by the New York Department of State.

What is the penalty for violating the license laws?

- A licensee who violates the license law may have his or her license suspended or revoked. Violations also constitute a misdemeanor.

What are the general rules for a resident New York licensee operating a real estate brokerage business in New York?

- Brokers must operate a principal place of business in New York.
- Brokers must display a readily identifiable sign that can be read from the sidewalk or displayed in an office building lobby.
- Advertisements must contain the name of the broker's firm.
- Each branch office must have a separate license.
- Brokers must maintain a separate escrow account to hold any money with which they are entrusted by others.
- Duplicate originals of all documents must be delivered to the persons who signed them, and all documents related to any real estate transaction must be kept on file for at least three years.

Who may collect a commission?

- Only a supervising broker may collect a commission.
- A broker may share a commission only with the broker's associated salespersons, associate brokers, or other licensed brokers.

■ KEY TERMS GLOSSARY

administrative discipline The use of reprimands and denial, suspension, or revocation of licenses by the DOS to enforce the license law, rules, and regulations.

apartment information vendor A specially licensed service provider who provides information and services to prospective tenants.

apartment sharing agent A professional who brings together roommates and house-mates.

Article 12-A The section of the New York State Real Property Law that relates to the licensing of real estate service providers.

Article 78 procedure The process by which an action of a governmental body may be contested.

associate broker A broker who chooses to work as a salesperson under the name and supervision of another broker.

blind ad An advertisement that does not indicate that it was placed by a real estate licensee.

commingling The illegal act of a real estate broker who mixes other people's money with his or her own personal funds.

continuing education The requirement that licensees fulfill at least 22½ hours of professional education courses every two year licensing period.

denial, suspension, or revocation of license The action of punishing violations of the license law by refusing to issue a license (*denial*), recalling a license temporarily (*suspension*), or permanently (*revocation*).

Department of State The state agency that supervises real estate licensees in New York.

escrow The closing of a transaction through a third party called an *escrow agent*, or *escrowee*, who receives certain funds and documents to be delivered upon the performance of certain conditions outlined in the escrow instructions.

irrevocable consent An agreement in which an out-of-state broker agrees that lawsuits may be brought against the broker in the state where he or she seeks a license.

kickback The act of returning a portion of a commission as a gift to buyers or sellers.

misdemeanor A crime greater than a violation but less serious than a felony.

mortgage banker Mortgage loan companies that originate, service, and sell loans to investors.

net listing A listing based on the net price the seller will receive if the property is sold. Under a net listing the broker can offer the property for sale at the highest price obtainable to increase the commission. This type of listing is illegal in many states.

pocket card A wallet-size copy of a real estate license, which must be carried by the licensee.

real estate broker A person, partnership, association or corporation that sells or offers to sell, buys or offers to buy, or negotiates the purchase, sale or exchange of real estate, or that leases (or offers to lease) or rents (or offers to rent) any real estate or improvements thereon for others and for a compensation or valuable consideration.

real estate salesperson A licensee who assists a licensed broker in the field of real estate.

REALTOR® A licensee who is also a member of the National Association of REALTORS®.

reciprocity An agreement between or among states to recognize each other's licensees, such as real estate salespersons or brokers.

revocation The act of rescinding a previously granted power of authority, such as power of attorney, a license or an agency.

sponsoring broker The principal broker in a firm who is responsible for training and supervising associated licensees.

suspension The temporary recall of a license.

termination of association notice A principal broker's notice to the Department of State that a licensee is no longer under his or her supervision.

violation An illegal act that is not as serious as a misdemeanor.

■ PASS-POINT CHECKLIST

- **Purpose of Real Estate License Laws**
  - Who Must Be Licensed
- **Qualifications for Licensure**
  - Education Requirements
- **License Examinations**
- **Licensing Procedure**
  - Fees
  - Issuing the License
- **Maintaining a License**
- **Termination or Changes in Association**
- **Renewal and Continuing Education**
- **Brokerage Management in Accordance with License Laws**
  - Obligations to Other Parties and Other Parties
- **Other Licenses or Registrations Involving Real Estate**
  - Licensing Nonresidents
- **Advertisements**
- **Suspension and Revocation of Licenses**
- **Unlicensed Real Estate Assistants**

■ PRACTICE QUESTIONS

1. The salesperson's license must be renewed
   a. every year.
   b. every four years.
   c. every third year.
   d. every two years.

2. A person who wants to receive a salesperson's license must have completed a qualifying course of how many hours?
   a. 18   c. 60
   b. 45   d. 90

3. All the following are requirements for obtaining a broker's license in New York, *EXCEPT*
   a. be a permanent resident of the United States.
   b. be 18 years old.
   c. have at least one full year's experience as a licensed salesperson.
   d. never have been convicted of a felony.

4. The broker's license is renewed
   a. every even year.
   b. every two years.
   c. once licensed, there is no need to renew.
   d. October 30, 2004, and every four years thereafter.

5. Gloria Jones closed her real estate office and went to EB White & Co. as the office manager. She is neither a partner nor corporate officer. She should be licensed as a(n)
   a. associate broker.
   b. sponsoring broker.
   c. salesperson.
   d. broker.

6. Broker Ben is a newly-licensed resident of New York. For tax and marketing purposes, he wants to have his office located in a shopping center in Pennsylvania, just across the border from his home. Is his plan permitted under New York's license law?
   a. Yes, if Ben's principal place of residence is located within five miles of the state border.
   b. Yes, if Ben posts a sign clearly indicating that he is licensed in the state of New York.
   c. No, because New York licensees may not practice in other states.
   d. No, every resident broker must maintain a principal place of business in New York.

7. How long must a broker keep documents relating to a transaction on file?
   a. Six months   c. Two years
   b. One year   d. Three years

8. In New York, who is entitled to collect commission on the sale of real estate?
   a. The supervising broker only
   b. Any associate broker
   c. Any salesperson
   d. The listing salesperson only

9. Which of the following is required to be contained in any advertisement for real property?
   a. The percentage commission split
   b. The name of the listing broker's firm
   c. The license number of any salespersons supervised by the broker who may be involved
   d. The date the listing expires

10. A violation of New York's laws, rules, and regulations governing the real estate profession is a
    a. felony.   c. misdemeanor.
    b. legal error.   d. business offense.

11. What is the term where a broker mixes his personal accounts with deposit funds from his clients?
    a. Illegal commingling
    b. Extra service
    c. Agency accountability
    d. Net listing

12. Broker blind ads that contain only a telephone number are
    a. economical.
    b. institutional advertising.
    c. advisable.
    d. prohibited.

13. Reciprocal licensing requires the salesperson to
    a. be licensed with a broker who has recropricity with that state.
    b. take the licensing courses required by the state they wish recropricity with.
    c. live in the state they want recropricity with.
    d. file a certificate of entitlement.

2

THE LAW OF AGENCY

■ TOPIC REVIEW

What is real estate brokerage?

- Real estate brokerage is the service of bringing together, for a fee or commission, people who wish to buy, sell, exchange, or lease real estate.
- Real estate brokerage is governed by the law of agency.

What is a real estate agent?

- A real estate agent is a person who is authorized to transact business on behalf of others. A real estate broker is an *agent* when he or she is authorized to sell real estate on behalf of a seller, or to assist a buyer in finding a suitable property. You work *for* the client. You work *with* a customer.

Who are the parties in an agency relationship?

- Whoever hires the broker, whether the buyer or the seller, is the *principal*. The principal is also known as the *client*.
- In a real estate transaction, the broker is the *agent* of a buyer, a seller, a landlord, or prospective tenant. A real estate salesperson is the broker's agent, and a *subagent* of the broker's principal, and owes the principal the same loyalties and duties as the broker.
- The relationship of trust and confidence between a principal and agent is known as a *fiduciary* relationship.

What is special about a fiduciary relationship?

- In a fiduciary relationship, the agent owes certain duties to the principal (CCLOAD):
  - Care
  - Confidentiality
  - Loyalty
  - Obedience
  - Accounting
  - Disclosure

■ An agent who breaches his or her fiduciary duties is exposed to loss of commission, loss of license, voiding of the transaction, and an adverse judgment in a lawsuit.

Does the agent owe the same duties to all parties?

■ No, the agent works for the principal and with the customer. An agent owes the principal (client) advice, counsel, and fiduciary duties, and must put the client's interests above all others. The customer is only entitled to fair and honest dealing.

Can a broker be the agent of both parties?

■ Yes, but only with the prior knowledge and consent of both parties. Such a relationship is known as *dual agency*.

What are the types of agency relationships?

■ An agent may be a universal, general, or special agent, depending on the scope of his or her authority to act on the principal's behalf.
■ A real estate broker is usually a special agent, authorized to represent the principal in one specific activity under detailed instructions.

How is an agency relationship created?

■ An agency relationship can be created *expressly* by either an oral or a written agency agreement between the principal and the agent, or *implied* from words or conduct. It can be created after the fact, by *ratification*, or by *estoppel* if someone relies on a representation that an agency relationship exists.

How is a broker typically compensated?

■ Compensation is always negotiable and should be based upon the broker's cost of doing business. Typically the fee is an agreed upon percentage of the sale price (commission) but set fees and sliding scales are not uncommon. Cooperating agents can be compensated by the listing broker or the client with the informed consent of all parties.

When is a commission earned by a broker?

■ The broker is the *procuring cause* when he brings about a *meeting of the minds* between the seller and a *ready, willing, and able buyer*. The essentials of a meeting of the minds are: Price; Amount of Cash; Duration of the Mortgages; Rate of Interest; and Amortization.

Does an agency relationship ever end?

■ An agency relationship may be terminated at any time due to the death or incompetence of either party; destruction of the property; expiration of its terms; mutual agreement; renunciation or revocation; bankruptcy; or fulfilment of the purpose for which the agency relationship was established.

■ KEY TERMS GLOSSARY

accountability An agent's fiduciary duty to account for any money involved in the transaction.

agency The relationship between a principal and an agent wherein the agent is authorized to represent the principal in certain transactions.

agency coupled with an interest An agency relationship in which the agent has an interest in the property.

agent One who is authorized to transact some business or to manage some affair for another.

brokerage The business of bringing buyers and sellers together in the marketplace.

buyer's broker A broker who has entered into an agreement to represent a buyer (the broker's principal and client) in finding a suitable property.

client The principal.

commission A broker's compensation for having successfully performed the service for which he or she was employed; usually percentage of the purchase price.

confidentiality The agent's fiduciary duty to keep a principal's information confidential.

customer The third party with whom the agent deals on behalf of the principal.

disclosure The requirement that a licensee clearly disclose for whom he or she is working, or requirements that prospective purchasers be informed of a property's condition.

dual agency The act of representing, or appearing to represent, both principals' interests simultaneously in the same transaction.

expressed agency A form of agency that is specifically stated, either orally or in writing.

fiduciary One in whom trust and confidence is placed; a reference to a broker employed under the terms of a listing contract or buyer agency agreement.

fiduciary duties The specific legal duties that are owed by an agent to a principal.

fiduciary relationship A relationship of trust and confidence between an agent and his or her principal.

fraud The intentional misrepresentation of a material fact in such a way as to harm or take advantage of another person.

general agent An agent who is empowered to represent the principal in a specific range of matters, and who may bind the principal to any contract within the scope of the agent's authority.

implied agency An agency relationship established by the action of the parties, not by any oral or written agreement.

informed consent Agreement based on full and fair disclosure of all facts necessary to make a rational decision.

kickbacks The return of part of the commission as gifts or money to buyers or sellers.

latent defects A hidden defect that is not discoverable by ordinary inspection.

law of agency The law that governs the relationships and duties of agents, clients, and customers.

listing agreement A written agreement that creates an agency relationship between a seller and a broker.

loyalty The fiduciary duty under which an agent puts the principal's interest above all others'.

meeting of the minds The agreement by the parties to a transaction on essential terms.

misrepresentation Falsely stating or concealing a material fact with the intent of causing another party to act.

obedience The agent's fiduciary duty to the principal

power of attorney A written instrument authorizing a person, the *attorney-in-fact*, to act as agent for another person to the extent indicated in the instrument.

principal An individual who hires and delegates to the agent the responsibility of representing his or her interests.

procuring cause of sale The status of a broker who produces a ready, willing, and able buyer, or who brings about a meeting of the minds.

puffing Statements of opinion that exaggerate a property's benefits.

ratification The creation of an agency relationship when a principal accepts (ratifies) the agent's conduct as that of an agent of the principal.

ready, willing, and able buyer A person who is (1) prepared to buy on the seller's terms, (2) is financially capable, and (3) is ready to take positive steps toward consummation of the transaction.

reasonable care The duty of a broker to properly perform his or her duties.

self-dealing The act of a broker who lists property and then buys it and collects the agreed-on commission.

special agent An agent who is authorized to represent the principal in one specific transaction or business activity under detailed instructions (a real estate broker is usually a special agent).

subagent Third party licensee working on behalf of another's client.

undisclosed dual agency The act of representing both principal parties in the same transaction without providing full written disclosure to the parties and receiving their consent.

undivided loyalty The fiduciary duty owed by an agent to the principal or client.

universal agent An individual who has authority to represent the principal in all matters that can be delegated.

■ PASS-POINT CHECKLIST

- ■ **What Is an Agent?**
  - ■ Types of Agents
- ■ **Creation of Agency**
- ■ **Agency and Brokerage**
  - ■ Seller as Principal
  - ■ Buyer as Principal
  - ■ Broker as Principal
  - ■ Importance of Agency Law to Licensees
  - ■ Basic Agency Relationships
- ■ **Fiduciary Responsibilities**
  - ■ Fiduciary Duties to the Principal
  - ■ Breach of Fiduciary Duties
  - ■ Scope of Authority
  - ■ Agent's Responsibilities to Other Parties in the Transaction
- ■ **The Broker's Compensation**
  - ■ Salesperson's Compensation
- ■ **Termination of Agency**

■ PRACTICE QUESTIONS

1. If a buyer retains a broker to represent him or her in locating real estate, the broker is the buyer's
   - **a.** principal.
   - **b.** employee.
   - **c.** agent.
   - **d.** client.

2. What is the relationship between a salesperson and the seller represented by the salesperson's supervising broker?
   - **a.** Independent contractor
   - **b.** Subagent
   - **c.** Agent
   - **d.** Principal

3. Which of the following best defines *Agency*?
   - **a.** The transaction of some business or management of some affair on behalf of another
   - **b.** Representing a principal in one specific transaction under detailed instructions
   - **c.** The production of a ready, willing, and able buyer or the bringing about a meeting of the minds in a real estate transaction
   - **d.** The bringing together, for a fee or commission, of people who wish to buy, sell, exchange, or lease real estate

4. Dual agency is permissible when
   a. it's the only way a broker can collect a commission.
   b. the informed consent of all parties have been given.
   c. the subagent wishes to purchase the property.
   d. the listing broker requires it.

5. The act of representing, or appearing to represent, the interests of both principals in the same transaction is referred to as
   a. fraud.
   b. self-dealing.
   c. dual agency.
   d. misrepresentation.

6. All of the following are characteristics of a ready, willing, and able buyer, *EXCEPT*
   a. prepared to buy on the seller's terms.
   b. ready to take positive steps toward the consummation of the transaction.
   c. willing to enter into a written representation agreement with a licensed broker.
   d. is financially capable of making a purchase.

7. Broker Betty signs a listing agreement with the owner of Lofty Manor, under which she will receive a 6 percent commission. Two days later, Betty buys the property from the seller for the full listed price and collects her 6 percent commission. Which of the following terms best describes this transaction?
   a. Kickback
   b. Self-dealing
   c. Agency coupled with an interest
   d. Fraud

8. An agent who has the authority to represent the principal in all matters that can be delegated is what kind of agent?
   a. Special   c. Unlimited
   b. General   d. Universal

9. If Salesperson Sam tells a prospective buyer about a very average property's "lovely view," "beautiful landscaping," and "fine architecture," in what activity is Sam engaging?
   a. Disclosure   c. Self-dealing
   b. Ratification   d. Puffing

10. An agent who is authorized to represent the principal in one specific transaction under detailed instructions is what kind of agent?
    a. Special   c. Limited
    b. General   d. Universal

11. Compensation is always
    a. based upon a percentage of the sales price.
    b. mutually negotiable.
    c. a set fee.
    d. paid by the seller.

12. A salesperson is compensated by
    a. the oil company who will pay a fee for the new buyer's name.
    b. the cooperating office.
    c. a satisfied broker.
    d. only the broker.

AGENCY AND REAL ESTATE BROKERAGE BUSINESS

■ TOPIC REVIEW

What are the types of agency relationships in New York?

■ An agency relationship may exist between a variety of different parties: between a broker and client, a broker and salespersons, or between two cooperating brokers.

■ Single agents represent only a single party—the buyer or the seller—in any one transaction.

■ Buyer agents, as their name implies, represent buyers (a buyer agent may be compensated by either the buyer or the seller, however).

■ Seller's agents act on behalf of the seller. A cooperating agent (or "selling agent") may specifically reject an agency relationship. Otherwise, the cooperating agent is usually assumed to be the seller's subagent.

■ A listing agent should obtain the seller's informed consent before creating a subagency through any kind of cooperative agreement with another broker.

■ A dual agent is a broker who represents both parties in a single transaction. Dual agency is strictly forbidden by New York's license law unless the buyer and the seller have both given their informed written consent. It is possible for a dual agency situation to arise inadvertently, without any intentional act. Some transactions are particularly risky for this type of accidental or implied dual agency: for instance, in-house sales, cooperating arrangement with buyer agents, and self-dealing.

What are the agency disclosure requirements in New York?

■ New York law requires full disclosure of agency relationships (RPL 443). Both brokers and salespersons must disclose the nature and extent of their relationships in writing at the first substantive contact with a prospective buyer or seller, and again when a listing or agency agreement is entered into.

The client must sign an acknowledgment that he or she has read and understood the disclosure form.

■ A seller's agent must also disclose and obtain the acknowledgment of prospective buyers or their agents at the first substantive contact with the party. Buyer agents must similarly provide disclosure to the seller or seller's agent.

■ KEY TERMS GLOSSARY

buyer agency An agency relationship in which the broker/agent represents the interests of the buyer.

dual agency An agency relationship in which the agent represents both principal parties in the same transaction (dual agency without full written disclosure to, and approval of, all parties is illegal in New York).

exclusive-agency listing A listing agreement in which the broker is entitled to a commission if the property is sold during the listing term, unless the seller, acting alone, procures a buyer.

exclusive right to represent The most common form of buyer agency agreement.

exclusive-right-to-sell listing A listing agreement in which the broker is entitled to a commission regardless of who procures the buyer.

first substantive contact The point at which agents must disclose and obtain signed acknowledgments of their agency relationships.

implied creation of a subagency The unintended creation of a fiduciary relationship through an informal cooperation arrangement between brokers.

informed consent Agreement to an act based on the full and fair disclosure of all the facts a reasonable person would need in order to make a rational decision.

In-House Sale The in-house sale is where one firm (including all the branch offices) lists and sells the same property. The agency relationship is determined by mutual agreement between the listing agent and seller and the selling agent and the buyer. If the buyer elects to have customer service, dual agency is not an issue. Dual agency does not occur unless both the buyer and seller elect to have client services and give informed consent to the relationships. Dual agency occurs only by the specific transaction.

listing broker The broker with whom a seller enters into a valid listing agreement for the sale of his or her real estate.

MLS Multiple Listing Service (MLS) is an information service whereby members share listings through an offer of cooperation made to other members.

Offer of Cooperation When the listing broker permits other agents to participate in the sale of property.

open listing The least restrictive type of listing agreement, in which the seller is free to employ any number of brokers and must pay a commission only to the broker who successfully produces a ready, willing and able buyer.

seller agency Traditional real estate agency, in which the broker represents the seller.

selling broker The broker who successfully finds a ready, willing, and able buyer for a property (may or may not be the listing broker).

single agency An agency relationship in which the agent represents a single party.

subagency An agency relationship in which the broker's sales associate, or a cooperating broker, assume a fiduciary duty to the principal who has designated the broker as an agent.

undisclosed dual agency Representation of both principal parties in the same transaction without full written disclosure to and approval of all parties.

vicarious liability A liability that arises because of the relationship between the liable person and other parties, not from any action.

■ PASS-POINT CHECKLIST

- **New York Agency Disclosure Requirements**
- **Agency Alternatives**
- **Subagency**
    - Creating a Subagency
- **Dual Agency**
    - Informed Consent
    - Undisclosed Dual Agency
- **Single Agency**
    - Handling In-House Sales
- **Designated Agency**
    - Handling Cooperative Sales
- **Agency Forms**
    - Listing Agreements
- **Buyer Agency**
    - Compensating Buyer Agents
    - Working Relationships with Buyers
    - Buyer-Agency Agreements
- **Types of Listings**
    - Exclusive-Right-to-Sell
    - Exclusive Agency
    - Open Listing

■ PRACTICE QUESTIONS

1. A New York real estate licensee may enter into any of the following types of listing agreements, *EXCEPT*
   a. open.
   b. single.
   c. net.
   d. exclusive-agency.

2. A single agent represents
   a. a buyer or a seller.
   b. a buyer and a seller, if disclosed in writing.
   c. sellers only.
   d. one or more parties in a transaction.

3. What must a listing agent do prior to entering into a cooperative agreement creating a subagency?
   a. Obtain the informed, written consent of all parties to the transaction
   b. Agree to a blanket unilateral offer of cooperation
   c. Ensure that he or she has signed an open listing agreement with the seller
   d. Obtain the informed consent of the seller

4. At what point is a licensee required to disclose the nature of his or her representation to a potential buyer or seller?
   a. At any time prior to closing
   b. Within ten days of the first substantive contact
   c. At the time of the first substantive contact
   d. A broker must make a disclosure; salespeople are not required to do so

5. Who may legally compensate a buyer agent?
   a. The seller only, from the proceeds of the sale
   b. The buyer or the seller
   c. Only the buyer may compensate his or her agent.
   d. Buyer agents are traditionally compensated by both principles to the transaction at the time of closing.

6. A seller's option to permit other brokers to participate in the sale without establishing a subagency relationship is a(n)
   a. blanket unilateral offer of subagency.
   b. exclusive-agency listing agreement.
   c. simple offer of cooperation.
   d. implied creation of subagency.

7. The most common form of buyer agency agreement is an
   a. implied buyer agency.
   b. exclusive right to represent.
   c. exclusive-agency agreement.
   d. exclusive-right-to-purchase agency agreement.

8. In-house sales, cooperating brokers who are buyer agents, and broker or salesperson self-dealing all pose a serious risk of
   a. implied subagency.
   b. undisclosed dual agency.
   c. net listings.
   d. single agency.

9. By which of the following listing agreements is the broker offered the least protection?
   a. Open
   b. Exclusive-right-to-sell
   c. Exclusive-agency
   d. Dual agency

10. Broker Bonnie signs a listing agreement with a seller, and a buyer agency agreement with a prospective purchaser. Both the seller and the prospective buyer sign written disclosure statements agreeing to this arrangement. What is this type of relationship called?
    a. Disclosed subagency
    b. Disclosed single agency
    c. Disclosed dual agency
    d. Dual exclusive agency

11. If the buyer is represented by a buyer's agent, the buyer's financial condition
   a. should be a confidential matter.
   b. is a material fact needed by the seller.
   c. should be discussed only by the attorney's preparing the contract.
   d. is immaterial.

12. A broker is not liable for material defects he did not know about.
   a. Incorrect—a broker and his agents are required to perform due diligence.
   b. This statement is correct.
   c. Only the engineer can disclose defects.
   d. If the seller forbids disclosure, the seller must comply.

13. First Substantive occurs when
   a. the buyer presents an offer.
   b. the seller accepts the offer.
   c. when office internet site is looked at.
   d. when the buyer or seller begin to discuss their specifics.

CHAPTER FOUR

ESTATES AND INTERESTS

■ TOPIC REVIEW

What is the difference among the terms "land," "real estate," and "real property"?

■ *Land* includes the surface of the earth as well as mineral deposits under the surface and the air space above it. Rights to the surface, mineral deposits, and air space may be held by different owners.

■ The term *real estate* includes land and man-made improvements attached to it.

■ *Real-property* includes real estate plus the bundle of legal rights.

How are bodies of water owned?

■ A landowner also has the right to use water on or adjacent to his or her property.

■ *Riparian rights* involve bodies of water such as rivers and streams. Owners of land adjacent to waterways that cannot be navigated (for instance, that are too shallow for a boat) also own the waterway to the center. Property owners whose land borders a navigable waterway own the property up to the high-water mark. The riverbed belongs to the state.

■ *Littoral rights* are held by owners of land that borders on large bodies of water, such as lakes and oceans. The adjacent landowner has use of the water and owns the land up to the high water mark.

What is a "fixture"?

■ Property that does not fall into the definition of *real estate* is *personal property,* also known as *chattels.*

■ When personal property is permanently attached to land, it may become a *fixture,* and be included as part of the real estate.

■ When a tenant installs personal property for some business or commercial purpose, however, the property is a *trade fixture,* and may be removed by the tenant when the lease expires.

What are the general-use classifications of real property?

■ Real property can be classified as residential, commercial, industrial, agricultural, or special-purpose.

What is an "estate"?

■ An *estate* is the kind of ownership interest someone holds. One way an estate may be defined is by time: *freehold estates*, for instance, may be held indefinitely. On the other hand, a *leasehold estate* (involving landlords and tenants) has a definite length.

■ Some estates may be inherited: fee simple, fee on condition, and qualified fee estates.

■ *Life estates* are granted for the life of the new owner or (in a *life estate pur autre vie*) for the life of a third party (called the measuring life).

■ When an estate expires, ownership may revert to the original owner (called *reverter*) or be passed on to a designated new owner (a *remainder*).

Are there special rules for married owners of real property in New York?

■ *Tenancy by the entirety* is a form of *joint tenancy* for property that is owned by a husband and wife. Unless the couple specifically state in the deed that they wish to own the property in some other manner, they will be presumed to own it by the entirety.

■ Neither party can force a sale of property held by the entirety by an action seeking partition.

■ Divorce automatically changes ownership by the entirety to a *tenancy in common*.

■ Homestead is *not* an estate in New York.

■ New York is *not* a community property state.

May title to real estate be held by more than one person at a time?

■ Property that is owned in *severalty* is held by one single owner.

■ When two or more persons not married to each other hold title to real estate, they own it as *tenants in common* unless their deed specifically states some other intention.

■ When property is owned in a *tenancy in common*, it is held by multiple owners at once. The shares may be unequal, and an individual owner has the right to sell his or her interest or leave it to his or her heirs or beneficiaries.

What makes joint tenancy different from a tenancy in common?

■ In a *joint tenancy*, there are two or more owners with the *right of survivorship*. When one owner dies, his or her share passes automatically to the remaining co-owner(s). The intent to create a joint tenancy with right of survivorship must be stated in the deed. Also, the *four unities* of possession, interest, time, and title must be present.

■ Tenants in common and joint tenants may force a sale of the property by partition.

How is title held in a trust?

- When real estate ownership is held in trust, the *trustor* (original owner) conveys title to the property to a *trustee*. The trustee administers the property on behalf of a *beneficiary*.

May business organizations own real estate?

- A corporation holds title to real estate in severalty.
- A partnership or limited liability company is entitled to hold title in its own name.
- A syndicate is an association formed for the purpose of making an investment. Some syndicates, called joint ventures, are organized only for the life of a single project.

What is the difference between a cooperative and a condominium?

- In a *cooperative* form of residential ownership, title to the property is held by a corporation. The corporation pays taxes, operating expenses and payments on the building's mortgage (if any) creates house rules and admission procedures. Depending upon the bylaws, Shareholders may or may not mortgage the individual units. Individual owners hold a share in the corporation and a long-terms lease to the unit he or she occupies. Owners pay monthly charges to cover expenses.
- In a *condominium*, each occupant is an owner of fee simple title to a living unit plus a proportionate share of the common areas. Each owner pays his or her own taxes, and is free to mortgage the unit.

■ KEY TERMS GLOSSARY

act of waste See *waste*.

agricultural real estate Farms, timberland, pasture land, and orchards.

air rights The right to use the open space above a property, generally allowing the surface to be used for another purpose.

bundle of legal rights The concept of land ownership that includes ownership of all legal rights to the land; for example, possession, control within the law, and enjoyment.

chattels Personal property such as household goods or fixtures.

commercial real estate Business property, including offices, shopping malls, theaters, hotels, and parking facilities.

common elements Parts of a property normally in common use by all of the condominium residents.

condominium The absolute ownership of an apartment or a unit (generally in a multiunit building) plus an undivided interest in the ownership of the common elements, which are owned jointly with the other condominium unit owners.

convey Transfer.

conveyance The transfer of title of land from one to another. The means or medium by which title to real estate is transferred.

cooperative A residential multiunit building whose title is held by a corporation owned by and operated for the benefit of persons living within the building, who are the stockholders of the corporation, each possessing a proprietary lease.

co-ownership Ownership by two or more persons.

corporation An entity or organization created by operation of law whose rights of doing business are essentially the same as those of an individual.

devise A gift of real property by will; the act of leaving real property by will.

emblements Annual crops of wheat, corn, vegetables, and fruit; generally considered personal property.

estate in land The degree, quantity, nature, and extent of interest a person has in real property.

fee simple The maximum possible estate or right of ownership of real property, continuing forever. Sometimes called a *fee* or *fee simple absolute*.

fixture An item of personal property that has been converted to real property by being permanently affixed to the realty.

freehold estates An estate in land in which ownership is for an indeterminate length of time, in contrast to a leasehold estate.

general partnership A typical form of joint venture in which each general partner shares in the administration, profits, and losses.

grant A sale or gift of real property.

homestead Land that is owned and occupied as the family home. The right to protect a portion of the value of this land from unsecured judgments for debts.

improvement Any structure erected on a site to enhance the value of the property, such as buildings, fences, driveways, curbs, sidewalks, or sewers.

industrial real estate Warehouses, factories, land in industrial districts and research facilities (sometimes referred to as *manufacturing property*).

interest Ownership.

joint tenancy Ownership of real estate between two or more parties who have been named in one conveyance as joint tenants. On the death of a joint tenant, his or her interest passes to the surviving joint tenant or tenants.

joint venture The joining of two or more people to conduct a specific business enterprise. A joint venture is similar to a partnership in that it must be created by agreement between the parties to share in the losses and profits of the venture. It is unlike a partnership in that the venture is for one specific project only, rather than for a continuing business relationship.

land The earth's surface, extending downward to the center of the earth and upward infinitely into space.

leasehold estates A tenant's right to occupy real estate during the term of a lease; generally considered personal property.

life estate An interest in real or personal property that is limited in duration to the lifetime of its owner or some other designated person or persons.

limited liability company A hybrid business entity that combines the managerial freedom of partnerships with the limited liability for owner and avoidance of income taxes offered by corporations.

limited partnership A partnership that is administered by one or more general partners and funded by limited or silent partners who are by law responsible for losses only to the extent of their investments.

littoral rights (1) A landowner's claim to use water in large navigable lakes and oceans adjacent to his or her property. (2) The ownership rights to land bordering these bodies of water up to the high-water mark.

parcel A specific piece of real estate.

partition The division of real property made between those who own it in undivided shares.

partnership An association of two or more individuals who carry on a continuing business for profit as co-owners.

personal property Items, called *chattels*, that do not fit into the definition of real property; movable objects.

real estate A portion of the earth's surface extending downward to the center of the earth and upward infinitely into space including all things permanently attached thereto, whether by nature or by a person.

real property Real estate plus all the interests, benefits, and rights inherent in ownership.

remainder interest The remnant of an estate that has been conveyed to take effect and be enjoyed after the termination of a prior estate, such as when an owner conveys a life estate to one party and the remainder to another (called the *remainderman* regardless of gender).

remainderman The individual named to receive property after a life tenant's death.

residential real estate All property used for housing, from acreage to small city lots, both single-family and multifamily, in urban, suburban, and rural areas.

reversionary interest The remnant of an estate that the grantor holds after he or she has granted a life estate to another person, if the estate will return, or revert, to the grantor; also called a *reverter*.

right of survivorship Characteristic of joint tenancy, the right by which a deceased joint tenant's interest passes to the surviving joint tenant or tenants.

riparian rights An owner's rights in land that borders on or includes a stream, river, lake, or sea. These rights include access to and use of the water.

severalty Ownership of real property by one person only; also called *sole ownership*.

sole proprietorship A business owned by one individual.

special-purpose real estate Religious institutions, schools, cemeteries, hospitals, and government-held land.

subsurface rights Ownership rights in a parcel of real estate of any water, minerals, gas, oil and so forth that lie beneath the surface of the property.

surface rights Ownership rights in a parcel of real estate that are limited to the surface of the property and do not include the air above it (air rights) or the minerals below the surface (subsurface rights).

syndicate A combination of people or firms formed to accomplish a joint venture.

tenancy by the entirety The joint ownership acquired by husband and wife during marriage. Upon the death of one spouse, the survivor becomes the owner of the property.

tenant in common A form of co-ownership by which each owner holds an undivided interest in real property as if he or she were sole owner. Each individual owner has the right to partition. Tenants in common have no right of survivorship.

title Evidence that the owner of land is in lawful possession thereof; evidence of ownership.

trade fixture Articles installed by a tenant under the terms of a lease and removable by the tenant before the lease expires.

trust A fiduciary arrangement whereby property is conveyed to a person or an institution, called a *trustee*, to be held and administered on behalf of another person, called a *beneficiary*.

trustee The person or institution who holds and administers trust property on behalf of another.

trustor The individual who establishes a trust.

undivided interest A partial interest in real estate that cannot be physically distinguished from other proportional interests in the same parcel.

unities of interest, possession, time, and title The four unities required to create a joint tenancy.

■ PASS-POINT CHECKLIST

- ■ **Real Estate Transactions**
- ■ **Land, Real Estate, and Real Property**
  - ■ Land
  - ■ Real Estate
  - ■ Real Property
- ■ **Real Property versus Personal Property**
  - ■ Fixtures
  - ■ Uses of Real Estate

- **Estate (Ownership) in Land**
  - Fee Simple Estate
  - Qualified Fee Estate
  - Fee on Condition
  - Life Estates

- **Forms of Ownership**
  - Severalty
  - Co-Ownership

- **Trusts**

- **Ownership of Real Estate by Business Organizations**
  - Partnerships
  - Corporations
  - Limited Liability Company
  - Syndicates

- **Cooperative and Condominium Ownership**
  - Cooperative Ownership
  - Condominium Ownership

- **Other Ways Title Is Transferred**

■ PRACTICE QUESTIONS

1. Which of the following includes both attached, man-made improvements and the bundle of legal rights?
   a. Land
   b. Real estate
   c. Real property
   d. Chattels

2. A property owner sold the rights to any oil or natural gas deposits to a refining company, and sold the right to grow soybeans to a farmer. Which of the following correctly states the ownership rights involved under these facts?
   a. The refining company owns the land, and the farmer owns the real estate.
   b. The refining company owns the subsurface rights, and the farmer owns the surface rights.
   c. The property owner continues to own the property in severalty.
   d. The farmer automatically acquires the air rights along with the right to farm the land.

3. If a parcel lies adjacent to a creek that is no more than three inches deep at its deepest point, what is the extent of the owner's rights to the waterway?
   a. He or she owns the creek to the high-water mark, but the bed belongs to the state of New York.
   b. He or she holds littoral rights to the high-water mark.
   c. He or she has riparian rights to the creek bed only.
   d. He or she has riparian rights to the middle of the waterway.

4. Personal property installed by a tenant for a business purpose is classified as a
   a. trade fixture.
   b. leasehold estate.
   c. chattel fixture.
   d. leasehold fixture.

5. Severalty of Ownership is
   a. many owners.
   b. husband and wife.
   c. granted through foreclosure.
   d. sole ownership.

6. Under which form of ownership must the four unities exist?
   a. Severalty
   b. Tenancy in common
   c. Joint tenancy
   d. Tenancy by the entirety

7. A form of ownership that is limited to property acquired by a married couple in New York is
   a. joint tenancy.
   b. tenancy by the entirety.
   c. tenancy in common.
   d. community property.

8. A joint venture organized for a single project is a common type of
   a. syndicate.
   b. partnership.
   c. limited liability company.
   d. corporation.

9. An owner has a share in the corporation that holds title to his apartment building, and a long-term lease to his living unit. What type of ownership is this?
   a. Condominium
   b. Cooperative
   c. Tenancy in common
   d. Timeshare

10. Property such as household goods is referred to as
    a. emblements.   c. chattels.
    b. real estate.   d. trade fixtures.

CHAPTER FIVE

LIENS AND EASEMENTS

■ TOPIC REVIEW

What are the four types of encumbrances against real estate?

- Liens
- Deed restrictions
- Easements
- Encroachments

What is a lien?

- A lien is a financial claim against a debtor's real and personal property.
- General liens cover all the debtor/owner's real and personal property. Specific liens cover only the one parcel of real estate described in the instrument that gave rise to the debt (that is, a mortgage, tax bill or contract).
- Liens are enforced by selling the property and distributing the proceeds to satisfy the unpaid debts (a court-ordered foreclosure).

How is the priority of liens determined?

- Real estate tax liens are paid first. After taxes, lien priority is established by the order in which they were recorded in the public records.

Are there different types of liens?

- Mortgage liens provide lenders with security for mortgage loans.
- A mechanics' lien protects those whose work has added value to the real estate, such as a general contractor, subcontractor, or supplier.
- A judgment is a court order (usually for some amount of money). Once it is docketed (filed) by the judgment creditor, it is a lien on all the debtor's real property in the county where it was filed. A judgment may be filed in any other county in the state.
- A *lis pendens* (notice of pendency of a law suit), is a recorded notice that a lawsuit is awaiting trial and that a judgment may be recorded against the property in the future.

■ Federal estate taxes and state inheritance taxes are general liens against property owned by a deceased person.

■ A vendor's lien is a claim by a seller against a buyer who has failed to pay the entire purchase price. A vendee's lien arises in the context of an installment contract. It is a claim by a buyer against a seller who has failed to convey title.

What is a deed restriction?

■ A deed restriction is placed on land by a seller in order to limit or control the future use of the property.

How does an easement work?

■ An easement is a permanent right to use someone else's land.

■ Easements appurtenant involve adjacent tracts of land. The tract that benefits from the easement is known as the dominant estate; the tract across which the easement runs is called the servient estate.

■ An easement in gross is a right that attaches to the easement owner, rather than benefitting a property. An easement granted to a utility company to build and maintain poles or wires is an example of an easement in gross.

What is the difference between an encroachment and a license?

■ An encroachment is the physical intrusion of an improvement onto some other owner's property.

■ A license is temporary permission, granted by an owner, to enter his or her property for a specific, limited purpose.

■ KEY TERMS GLOSSARY

adverse possession The actual, open, notorious, hostile, and continuous possession of another's land under a claim of title. Possession for a statutory period may be a means of acquiring title.

Affidavit of Entitlement to Commission Real Property Law permits a broker to enter an Affidavit of Entitlement to Commission into the public records. It is public notice that a commission is due but it is not a lien on the property.

appurtenant A right, privilege, or improvement belonging to, and passing with, the land.

cloud on the title Any document, claim, unreleased lien, or encumbrance that may impair the title to real property or make the title doubtful; usually revealed by a title search and removed by either a quitclaim deed or suit to quiet title.

corporation franchise tax Tax levied on corporations as a condition of allowing them to do business in New York state.

deed restrictions An imposed restriction in a deed for the purpose of limiting the use of the land by future owners.

dominant estate A property that includes in its ownership the right to use an easement over another person's property for a specific purpose.

easement A right to use the land of another for a specific purpose, as for a right-of-way or utilities; an incorporeal interest in land.

easement appurtenant An easement involving adjacent parcels that runs with the land (is permanently attached), so that subsequent owners are bound by it, and it passes with the land.

easement by condemnation An easement created by the government or government agency that has exercised its right under eminent domain.

easement by grant An easement by one owner to another.

easement by necessity An easement allowed by law as necessary for the full enjoyment of a parcel of real estate; for example, a right of ingress and egress over a grantor's land.

easement by prescription An easement acquired by continuous, open, uninterrupted, exclusive, and adverse use of the property for the 10-year period prescribed by New York law.

easement in gross An easement that is not created for the benefit of any land owned by the owner of the easement but that attaches personally to the easement owner.

encroachment A building or some portion of it (a wall or fence, for instance) that extends beyond the land of the owner and illegally intrudes on land of an adjoining owner.

encumbrance Any claim by another (such as a mortgage, a tax or judgment lien, an easement, an encroachment, or a deed restriction) that may diminish the value of a property.

estate taxes Federal tax levied on property transferred upon death.

general lien The right of a creditor to have all of a debtor's property, both real and personal, sold to satisfy a debt.

involuntary lien A lien imposed against property without consent of the owner (such as a tax lien).

judgment The formal decision of a court upon the respective rights and claims of the parties to an action or suit. After a judgment has been entered and recorded with the county recorder, it usually becomes a general lien on the property of the defendant.

license The revocable permission for a temporary use of land.

lien A right given by law to certain creditors to have their debt paid out of the property of a defaulting debtor, usually by a court sale.

lis pendens (*notice of pendency*) A recorded legal document giving constructive notice that an action affecting a property has been filed.

mechanic's lien A statutory lien created in favor of contractors, laborers and material suppliers who have performed work or furnished materials adding to a property's value.

mortgage lien A lien or charge on the property of a mortgagor that secures the underlying debt obligations.

notice of pendency/lis pendens A recorded legal document giving constructive notice that an action affecting a particular property has been filed in either a state or a federal court.

party wall A wall that is located on or at a boundary line between two adjoining parcels of land and is used by both owners.

priority The order of position or time; the order in which documents or claims are filed and are entitled to be satisfied.

right-of-way The right given by one landowner to another to pass over the land, construct a roadway, or use as a pathway, without actually transferring ownership.

servient estate Land on which an easement exists in favor of an adjacent property (the *dominant estate*).

specific lien A lien affecting or attaching only to a certain parcel of land or piece of property.

subordination agreement Relegation to a lesser position in respect to a right or security.

tax lien A charge against property, created by operation of law. Tax liens and assessments take priority over all other liens.

voluntary lien A lien created by the owner's voluntary action, such as a mortgage.

■ PASS-POINT CHECKLIST

- ■ **Encumbrances**
- ■ **Liens**
- ■ **Effects of Liens on Title**
  - ■ Priority of Liens
- ■ **Liens Other Than Real Estate Taxes**
  - ■ Mortgage Liens
  - ■ Mechanic's Liens
  - ■ Other Liens
- ■ **Deed Restrictions**
- ■ **Easements**
  - ■ Easement Appurtenant
  - ■ Easement in Gross
  - ■ Easement by Necessity
  - ■ Easement by Prescription
  - ■ Party Walls
  - ■ Encroachments
  - ■ Licenses

■ PRACTICE QUESTIONS

1. When does a creditor's judgment become a lien on the debtor's real property?
   a. At the time the suit is filed
   b. When the judgment is docketed
   c. When the foreclosure sale is ordered
   d. When a lis pendens is filed

2. A vendor's lien is a
   a. seller's claim against a purchaser under an installment contract for failure to convey title.
   b. purchaser's claim against a seller under an installment contract.
   c. seller's claim against a purchaser.
   d. purchaser's claim against a vendee.

3. In an easement appurtenant, the tract that is benefited is referred to as the
   a. servient estate.
   b. dominant estate.
   c. gross estate.
   d. encumbered estate.

4. Temporary permission to enter another's property for a specific purpose is a(n)
   a. easement.
   b. encumbrance.
   c. permissive estate.
   d. license.

5. All of the following are true of an easement appurtenant, *EXCEPT*
   a. it is a permanent right.
   b. it involves adjacent parcels.
   c. the easement conveys with the land.
   d. it attaches personally to the easement owner.

6. A wall or fence that unlawfully extends onto an adjacent owner's property is a(n)
   a. easement in gross.
   b. encroachment.
   c. involuntary lien.
   d. easement by necessity.

7. Which type of easement may be acquired through the continuous, open, uninterrupted exclusive, and adverse use of a property for a certain period of time?
   a. Easement by prescription
   b. Easement in gross
   c. Easement by necessity
   d. Easement appurtenant

8. A creditor who voluntarily accepts a later priority position in favor of another creditor has probably entered into a(n)
   a. voluntary lien.
   b. lis pendens.
   c. subordination agreement.
   d. specific lien agreement.

9. What is the principal requirement of a federal estate tax lien and a state inheritance tax lien?
   a. The property must not be subject to any deed restrictions.
   b. The property must be sold at a foreclosure sale.
   c. The owner must be deceased.
   d. The owner must voluntarily create the lien.

10. Which of the following liens depends on value having been added to the real estate involved?
    a. Mechanic's lien
    b. Tax lien
    c. Judgment lien
    d. Mortgage lien

CHAPTER **6** SIX

REAL ESTATE INSTRUMENTS: DEEDS

■ TOPIC REVIEW

What is a metes-and-bounds description?

■ A metes-and-bounds description uses the physical location of monuments to describe an enclosed tract. The property's boundary line always ends back at the point of beginning.

What is a recorded plat of subdivision?

■ A recorded plat of subdivision subdivides land into lots. The subdivision map (plat) identifies the size and location of lots and streets. The map is filed in the recorder's office of the county in which the land described in the plat is located.

How are legal descriptions certified?

■ The usual method of certifying a legal description is by a survey. Mortgage and construction lenders often require surveys.

How are air rights and vertical elevations described?

■ The Geodetic Survey datum (mean sea level in New York Harbor) is the customary tool for describing air lots, condominium properties, and other vertical elevations.
■ Many larger cities have their own local datums linked to local geographic features. Other reference points, called benchmarks, further supplement and refine the description of vertical elevations based on datums.

What is a deed, and who are the parties involved?

■ A deed is the device by which an owner voluntarily transfers title. The owner (grantor) executes (signs) the deed and delivers it to the purchaser (donee), called the grantee.

What are the requirements for a valid deed?

- The grantor must have legal capacity to make a contract.
- The grantee must be readily identifiable.
- Granting clause, a legal description of the property being conveyed, and a recital of consideration must be included.
- Statement of exceptions and reservations must be included.
- The grantor's signature.
- Acknowledgment before a notary public or other officer is evidence of the validity of the grantor's signature.

When does title pass?

- Title passes when the grantor delivers the deed to the grantee, and the grantee accepts the deed.

What are the different types of deeds?

- General warranty deed: provides the most protection for grantees because it binds the grantor to five specific covenants (warranties)—seisin, quiet enjoyment, further assurances, and warranty forever.
- Bargain and sale deed with covenant: warrants that the grantor has not encumbered the real estate while he or she owned it.
- Bargain and sale deed without covenant: carries no warranties, although it implies that the grantor actually has legal title.
- Quitclaim deed: provides the least protection for grantees because it includes absolutely no warranties or implications. It conveys only the interest the grantor actually possesses.

■ KEY TERMS GLOSSARY

accession Acquiring title to additions or improvements to real property as a result of the annexations of fixtures or the accretion of alluvial deposits along the banks of streams.

alluvion Soil deposited on a shore due to the action of water.

attorney-in-fact A person who has been given a power of attorney on behalf of a grantor. The power must be recorded, and ends on the death of the grantor.

avulsion The sudden tearing away of land, as by earthquake, flood, volcanic action, or the sudden change in the course of a stream.

bargain and sale deed A deed that carries with it no warranties against liens or other encumbrances but that does imply that the grantor has the right to convey title.

bargain and sale deed with covenant A deed in which the grantor guarantees title against defects arising during the period of his or her tenure and ownership of the property but not against defects existing before that time.

benchmark A permanent reference mark or point established for use by surveyors in measuring differences in elevation.

consideration   Something received by the grantor in exchange for a deed.

conveyance   A term used to refer to any document that transfers title to real property. The term is also used in describing the act of transferring.

covenants   Agreements written into deeds and other instruments promising performance or nonperformance of certain acts.

datum   Point from which elevations are measured: mean sea level in New York harbor, or local datums.

dedication/dedication by deed   The voluntary transfer of private property by the owner to the public for some public use, such as for streets or schools.

deed   A written instrument that, when executed and delivered, conveys title to or interest in real estate.

delivery and acceptance   Transfer of possession of a thing from one person to another.

description   A specific, legal definition of a subject property.

devise   A gift of real property by will. The owner is the devisor, the recipient the devisee.

escheat   The reversion of property to the state or county, as provided by state law, in cases where a decedent dies intestate without heirs capable of inheriting, or when the property is abandoned.

executor/executrix   A person, corporate entity or other type of organization designated in a will to carry out its provisions.

full covenant and warranty deed title   A deed that provides the greatest protection, in which the grantor makes five legal promises (covenants of seisin, quiet enjoyment, further assurances, warranty forever against encumbrances) that the grantee's ownership will be unchallenged.

grantee   A person who receives a conveyance of real property from the grantor.

grantor   The person transferring title to or an interest in real property to a grantee.

intestate   The condition of a property owner who dies without leaving a valid will. Title to the property will pass to the decedent's heirs as provided in the state law of descent.

involuntary/voluntary alienation   The act of transferring property to another. Alienation may be voluntary, such as by gift or sale, or involuntary, as through eminent domain or adverse possession.

legal description   A description of a specific parcel of real estate complete enough for an independent surveyor to locate and identify it.

metes-and-bounds   A legal description using the boundaries and measurements of the land in question.

monument   A fixed natural or artificial object used to establish real estate boundaries for a metes-and-bounds description.

plat A map of a town, section, or subdivision indicating the boundaries of properties.

point (place) of beginning In a metes-and-bounds legal description, the starting point of the survey, situated in one corner of the parcel.

probate A legal process by which a court determines who will inherit a decedent's property and what the estate's assets are.

quitclaim deed A conveyance by which the grantor transfers whatever interest he or she has in the real estate, if any, without warranties.

rectangular survey system A system established in 1785 by the federal government for surveying and describing land outside the 13 original colonies by reference to principal meridians and base lines. Not used in New York.

referee's deed The deed delivered when property is conveyed under a court order.

reference to a plat A legal description that identifies properties as map locations.

seisin The possession of land by one who claims to own at least an estate for life therein.

special warranty deed A deed in which the grantor warrants, or guarantees, the title only against defects arising during the period of his or her tenure and ownership of the property and not against defects existing before that time.

survey The process by which boundaries are measured and land areas are determined; the on-site measurement of lot lines, dimensions, and position of a house on a lot, including the determination of any existing encroachments or easements.

testate Having made and left a valid will.

testator A person who has made a valid will. A woman is often referred to as a testatrix, although testator can be used for either gender.

title Evidence that the owner of land is in lawful possession thereof; evidence of ownership.

warranty deed A deed in which the grantor fully warrants good clear title to the premises.

■ PASS-POINT CHECKLIST

- **Legal Descriptions**
  - Metes and Bounds
  - Rectangular (Government Survey System)
  - Recorded Plat of Subdivision
  - Preparation and Use of a Survey

- **Measuring Elevations**
  - Air Lots
  - Datum
  - Condominium

- **Deeds**
  - Requirements for a Valid Conveyance
  - Execution of Corporate Deeds
  - Types of Deeds
- **Dedication by Deed**
- **Natural Processes**
- **Conveyance after Death**

PRACTICE QUESTIONS

1. Which of the following methods of legal description uses monuments and a point of beginning?
   a. Rectangular (government) survey
   b. Metes-and-bounds
   c. Recorded plat of subdivision
   d. Geodetic Survey

2. A referee's deed contains
   a. full covenant and warrantees.
   b. only warrantees.
   c. no covenants or warrantees.
   d. title guarantees.

3. Which of the following is used to compute vertical elevations for air lots and condominium descriptions?
   a. Rectangular (government) survey
   b. Metes-and-bounds
   c. Recorded plat of subdivision
   d. Geodetic Survey

4. The property of an owner who dies without leaving a will is conveyed by the law of
   a. testamentary succession.
   b. reference to a plat.
   c. delivery.
   d. intestacy.

5. All of the following are requirements for a valid deed, *EXCEPT*
   a. an identifiable grantee.
   b. recital of consideration.
   c. granting clause.
   d. recital of warranties and covenants.

6. Which of the following deeds provides a grantee with the greatest protection?
   a. General warranty
   b. Bargain and sale
   c. Quitclaim
   d. Special warranty

7. A deed in which the grantor guarantees title against defects arising only during the period of his or her ownership is what type of deed?
   a. General warranty
   b. Bargain and sale
   c. Quitclaim
   d. Special warranty

8. Which of the following deeds provides a grantee with the least protection?
   a. General warranty
   b. Bargain and sale
   c. Quitclaim
   d. Special warranty

9. How many acres are there in one square mile?
   a. 6   c. 64
   b. 36   d. 640

10. Which of the following deeds carries no warranties, but implies that the grantor holds title?
    a. General warranty
    b. Quitclaim
    c. Bargain and sale
    d. Bargain and sale with covenant

CHAPTER SEVEN

REAL ESTATE INSTRUMENTS: LEASES

■ TOPIC REVIEW

What is a lease?

■ A lease is an agreement granting one party the right to use another's property for a period of time in exchange for some valid consideration.

What constitutes a valid lease?

■ Legal capacity of the parties
■ A demising clause
■ Description of premises
■ Statement of terms and rent
■ Signatures of the parties
■ Many leases include a recital of the rights and obligations of the landlord and tenant, limitations on how the property may be used and provisions governing subletting, judgments, maintenance, and termination.

Is a lease an ownership estate?

■ A leasehold is classified as personal property, rather than as a real property interest.
■ A leasehold estate is an estate for years if it has a specific length of time.
■ A leasehold that runs for an indefinite period (such as year to year or month to month leases) is a periodic tenancy. A tenancy at will is a periodic tenancy.

Does New York law require that all leases be in writing to be valid?

■ In New York, the statute of frauds requires that any lease for a period longer than one year must be in writing to be enforceable. An oral lease, however, is valid if it involves a period of one year or less. If properly acknowledged, a lease for three years or more may be recorded in the public records.

Do all landlords have to keep tenant security deposits in an interest-bearing account?

■ Owners of six or more residential units are required by law to hold tenant security deposits in an interest-bearing account in a New York bank. All interest, less a one percent fee, is payable to the tenant.

Do tenants have a right to sublet?

■ Under New York law, tenants in any building with four or more residential units have the right to sublet.

■ A qualified tenant who wishes to sublet a unit must first obtain the landlord's consent. However, the landlord may not unreasonably withhold his or her consent to a sublet.

What events will terminate a lease?

■ Expiration of the lease period
■ Mutual agreement of the parties
■ Breach of the terms of the lease by either party
■ A lease is *NOT* terminated by the death of the tenant or the sale of the rented property.

What legal remedies are available to a landlord and a tenant?

■ If a tenant defaults on any lease provision, the landlord is entitled to sue for: (1) a money judgment; or (2) actual eviction if the tenant improperly retains possession of the premises.

■ If the rented premises become uninhabitable (because of the landlord's negligence or for any other reason), the tenant may withhold rent until such time as the condition is resolved.

■ KEY TERMS GLOSSARY

actual eviction Action in which a defaulted tenant is physically ousted from rented property pursuant to a court order.

assignment The transfer in writing of interest in a bond, mortgage, lease or other instrument.

constructive eviction Landlord actions that so materially disturb or impair the tenant's enjoyment of the leased premises that the tenant is effectively forced to move out and terminate the lease without liability for any further rent.

estate for years An interest for an exact period of time in property leased for a specified consideration.

graduated lease A lease that provides for a periodic change in the amount of rent to be paid.

gross lease A lease of property under which a landlord pays all property charges regularly incurred through ownership, such as repairs, taxes, and insurance.

ground lease A long-term lease of land only, on which the tenant usually owns a building or is required to build as specified in the lease; the tenant's rights and obligations continue until the lease expires or terminates.

holdover tenancy A tenancy in which a lessee retains possession of leased property after his or her lease has expired and the landlord, by continuing to accept rent, agrees to the tenant's continued occupancy.

implied warranty of habitability A legal theory in which a landlord renting residential property implies that the property is habitable and fit for its intended use.

index lease A lease in which the rent is periodically based on the government's cost-of-living index.

lease A written or oral contract between a lessor and a lessee that transfers the right to exclusive possession and use of the landlord's real property to the lessee for a specified period of time and for a stated consideration (rent).

leasehold estate A tenant's right to occupy real estate during the term of a lease; generally considered personal property.

lessee Tenant.

lessor Landlord.

month-to-month tenancy A periodic tenancy; that is, the tenant rents for one period at a time In the absence of a rental agreement (oral or written), a tenancy is generally considered to be month to month.

net lease A lease requiring the tenant to pay not only rent but also some or all costs of maintaining the property, including taxes, insurance, utilities, and repairs.

New York General Obligations Law New York's Statute of Frauds, which requires that agreements regarding the sale of real estate must be in writing.

percentage lease A lease commonly used for commercial property whose rental is based on the tenant's gross sales at the premises.

periodic estate An interest in property that continues from period to period: week to week, month to month, or year to year.

proprietary lease A lease given by the corporation that owns a cooperative apartment building to the shareholder for the shareholder's right as tenant to an individual apartment.

quiet enjoyment An owner's or possessor's right to use the property without interference.

security deposit A payment by a tenant, held by the landlord during the lease term and kept (wholly or partially) on default or destruction of the premises by the tenant.

statute of frauds The part of a state law that requires certain instruments, such as deeds, real estate sales contract and certain leases, to be in writing to be legally enforceable.

sublease Lease of premises by a tenant to a third party for part of the remaining lease term.

suit for possession A lawsuit initiated by a landlord to evict a tenant from leased premises after the tenant has breached one of the terms of the lease or has held possession of the property after the lease's expiration.

tenancy at sufferance An estate that arises when a tenant continues to occupy the premises after the lease has expired, without the landlord's consent.

tenancy at will An indefinite-term estate that gives the lessee the right to possession until the estate is terminated by either party.

■ PASS-POINT CHECKLIST

- ■ **Leasing Real Estate**
- ■ **Leasehold Estates**
  - ■ Estate for Years
  - ■ Periodic Estate
  - ■ Tenancy at Will
  - ■ Tenancy at Sufferance
- ■ **Typical Lease Provisions**
  - ■ Use of Premises
  - ■ Term of Lease
  - ■ Security Deposits
- ■ **Legal Principles of Leases**
  - ■ Lead Paint Notification
  - ■ Improvements
  - ■ Maintenance of Premises
  - ■ Assignment and Subleasing
  - ■ Apartment Sharing
  - ■ Renewals
  - ■ Termination of Lease
  - ■ Breach of Lease
- ■ **Pro-Tenant Legislation**
- ■ **Types of Leases**
  - ■ Gross Lease
  - ■ Net Lease
  - ■ Percentage Lease
  - ■ Other Lease Types

■ PRACTICE QUESTIONS

1. A leasehold estate that runs for an indefinite period of time creates a(n)
   a. estate for years.
   b. periodic lease.
   c. tenancy at sufferance.
   d. gross lease.

2. All of the following are requirements for any valid lease, *EXCEPT*
   a. a demising clause.
   b. description of the premises.
   c. a written document.
   d. statement of terms.

3. In New York, an oral lease is valid if it is for a period of
   a. one year or less.
   b. one year or more.
   c. three years or less.
   d. oral leases are invalid.

4. New York requires that an owner hold tenants' security deposits in an interest bearing New York bank account if he or she owns how many residential units?
   a. Three
   b. Four or more
   c. Six or fewer
   d. Six or more

5. All of the following events will terminate a lease, *EXCEPT*
   a. the death of the tenant.
   b. expiration of the lease period.
   c. breach of a lease term.
   d. mutual agreement of the parties.

6. The physical removal of a defaulted tenant from rented property is referred to as
   a. constructive eviction.
   b. tenancy at sufferance.
   c. actual eviction.
   d. breach of lease.

7. A week-to-week lease is an example of a
   a. ground lease.   c. estate for years.
   b. periodic lease.   d. tenancy at will.

8. A lease in which the landlord pays all property charges and the tenant pays only periodic rent is a
   a. gross lease.
   b. net lease.
   c. percentage lease.
   d. ground lease.

9. A commercial lease in which the periodic rental is based on the tenant's gross sales is a
   a. gross lease.
   b. net lease.
   c. percentage lease.
   d. ground lease.

10. A lease in which the tenant pays a fixed monthly rental as well as a percentage of maintenance costs, property tax, and insurance is a
    a. gross lease.
    b. net lease.
    c. percentage lease.
    d. ground lease.

CHAPTER EIGHT

8

REAL ESTATE INSTRUMENTS: CONTRACTS

■ TOPIC REVIEW

What is a contract?

■ A contract is an agreement between competent parties, supported by adequate consideration, involving some lawful action or activity.

How are contracts classified?

■ *Express*: the intention of the parties is clearly stated.
■ *Implied*: the agreement is demonstrated by the parties' actions.
■ *Bilateral*: both parties are obligated to act.
■ *Unilateral*: one party is required to perform only after the other party completes their contractual obligations.
■ *Legal enforceability*: a contract may be valid, void, voidable, or unenforceable.

What is the difference between an executed and an executory contract?

■ An executed contract has been fully performed by the parties.
■ An executory contract is one in which some term remains to be fulfilled or some act must still be performed. Also known as a conditional contract.

What are the characteristics of a valid contract?

■ Competent parties
■ Offer and acceptance
■ Consideration
■ Legality of object
■ Agreement in writing
■ Signed by the parties

How may a party to a contract transfer his or her rights and obligations to another?

■ Assignment: the written transfer of a party's interest in an existing contract to another, who steps into the original party's position

■ Novation: the substitution of a new contract or parties in place of the original

What legal remedies are available to an injured party in the event of a default?

■ The injured party may sue for monetary damages to cover the loss.

■ Alternatively, the injured party may sue for specific performance of the contract, forcing the defaulting party to complete the transaction.

■ A court order may be obtained forcing the defaulting party to comply with the contract.

What are the characteristics of a real estate sales contract?

■ A real estate sales contract brings together a buyer and seller to convey ownership of real estate. The buyer promises to purchase the property for the agreed-on price, and the seller promises to deliver good title as defined in the agreement.

What is the difference between an option agreement and a land contract?

■ In an option agreement, the optionee purchases the exclusive right, for a specific period of time, to buy or lease the optionor's property. The option may or may not be exercised during the option period.

■ In a land contract (also called an installment contract), the purchaser buys the seller's property over time. Although the buyer takes possession of the property, and is responsible for it, he or she does not receive the deed until the purchase price has been fully paid.

■ KEY TERMS GLOSSARY

agreement in writing and signed The statute of frauds' requirement for enforceability of certain types of contracts, including contracts for the sale of real estate, listing contracts, and leases for more than one year; a promise that is not in the written contract may not be legally binding (the parole evidence rule).

"as is" Words in a contract that indicate that the seller is making no guarantee or warranty about the property.

assignment The transfer in writing of interest in a bond, mortgage, lease or other instrument.

bilateral contract A contract in which both parties promise to do something; an exchange of promises.

breach of contract Violation of any terms or conditions in a contract without legal excuse; for example, failure to make a payment when it is due.

competent parties Those recognized by law as being able to contract with others; usually those of legal age and sound mind.

consideration Something of value that induces a person to enter into a contract. Consideration may be valuable (money) or good (love and affection).

contingency A provision in a contract that requires a certain act to be done or a certain event to occur before the contract becomes binding.

contract An agreement entered into by two or more legally competent parties by the terms of which one or more of the parties, for a consideration, undertakes to do or refrain from doing some legal act or acts.

counteroffer A new offer made as a reply to an offer received.

disclosure regarding agency relationships (form 443) Requires this fully completed form to be incorporated or included in the contract of sale or lease.

earnest money deposit Money deposited by a buyer under the terms of a contract, to be applied to the purchase price if the sale is closed.

equitable title The interest held by a vendee under a land contract or an installment contract; the equitable right to obtain absolute ownership to property when legal title is held in another's name.

escape clause A provision in a contract that allows one party to unilaterally void the contract without penalty; for instance, a seller may be allowed to look for a more favorable offer, while the purchaser retains the right to drop all contingencies or void the contract if another offer is received.

executed contract A contract in which all parties have fulfilled their promises and thus performed the contract.

executory contract (conditional) A contract under which something remains to be done by one or more of the parties.

express contract An oral or written contract in which the parties state the contract's terms and express their intentions in words.

forbearance A legal promise to perform some act.

implied contract A contract under which the agreement of the parties is demonstrated by their acts and conduct.

laches An equitable doctrine used by courts to bar a legal claim or prevent the assertion of a right because of undue delay or failure to assert the claim or right.

land contract A contract for the sale of real estate in which the purchase price is paid in periodic installments and the purchaser is in possession of the property even though title is retained by the seller until final payment. Also called an installment contract or contract for deed.

lead paint disclosure Required in all residential contracts for sale or leases.

legality of object The requirement that a valid and enforceable contract may not involve an illegal purpose or one that is against public policy.

liquidated damages An amount of money, agreed to in advance, that will serve as the total compensation due to the injured party if the other does not comply with the contract's terms.

memorandum of sale A nonbinding information sheet prepared by brokers in some New York localities that states the essential terms of the agreement; the final contract is later drawn up by an attorney.

novation Substituting a new obligation for an old one or substituting new parties to an existing obligation.

offer and acceptance Two essential components of a valid contract; a meeting of the minds when all parties agree to the exact terms.

option An agreement to keep open for a set period an offer to sell or purchase property.

parol evidence rule A rule of evidence providing that a written agreement is the final expression of the agreement of the parties, not be varied or contradicted by prior or contemporaneous oral or written negotiations.

real estate sales contract A contract for the sale of real estate, in which the purchaser promises to pay the agreed purchase price, and the seller agrees to deliver title to the property.

release The act or writing by which some claim or interest is surrendered to another.

rescission The act of canceling a contract.

rider Any amendment or attachment to a contract.

right of first refusal A deed restriction, a homeowner's condominium, or coopera-tive association's right to purchase property after a deal has been struck with another.

specific performance A legal action brought in a court of equity in special cases to compel a party to carry out the terms of a contract.

statute of frauds The part of state law requiring that certain instruments, such as deeds, real estate sales contracts, and certain leases, be in writing to be legally enforceable.

statute of limitations The law pertaining to the period of time within which certain actions must be brought to court; in New York, six years for contracts.

time is of the essence A phrase in a contract that requires the performance of a certain act within a stated period of time.

unenforceable contract A contract that seems on the surface to be valid, yet neither party can sue the other to force performance.

Uniform Commercial Code A codification of commercial law, adopted in most states, that attempts to make uniform all laws relating to commercial transactions, including chattel mortgages and bulk transfers. Security interests in chattels are created by an instrument known as a security agreement. To give notice of the security interest an financing statement must be recorded. Article 6 of the code regulates bulk transfers—the sale of a business as a whole including all fixtures, chattels, and merchandise.

unilateral contract A one-sided contract in which one party makes a promise so as to induce a second party to do something. The second party is not legally bound to perform; however, if the second party does comply, the first party is obligated to keep the promise. An open listing is an example of a unilateral contract.

valid contract A contract that complies with all the essentials of a contract and is binding and enforceable on all parties to it.

voidable contract A contract that seems to be valid on the surface but that may be rejected or disaffirmed by one of the parties.

void contract A contract that has no legal force or effect because it does not meet the essential elements of a contract.

■ PASS-POINT CHECKLIST

- **Contract Law**
  - Express and Implied Contracts
  - Bilateral and Unilateral Contracts
  - Executed and Executory Contacts
  - Validity of Contracts
  - Elements Essential to a Valid Contract
  - Performance of Contract
  - Assignment and Novation
  - Discharge of Contract
  - Default-Breach of Contract
  - Disclosures
    - Lead
    - Agency
    - Property Condition

- **Contracts Used in the Real Estate Business**
  - Broker's Authority to Prepare Documents
  - Listing Agreements
  - Sales Contacts
  - Head Cooperative Apartment Contracts
  - Condominium Sales
  - Option Agreements
  - Land Contracts
  - Local Forms
  - Recision

■ PRACTICE QUESTIONS

1. A contract in which one party has an obligation to perform some act only if the other party acts is a(n)
   a. executory contract.
   b. bilateral contract.
   c. unilateral contract.
   d. agreement, but not a contract.

2. The transfer by one party of his or her rights or obligations under a contract by substituting a new contract is a legal action known as
   a. assignment.
   b. release.
   c. novation.
   d. specific performance.

3. What is the statute of limitations in New York for a legal action based on a contract?
   a. One year   c. Six years
   b. Three years   d. Eight years

4. An agreement in which a buyer purchases a seller's real estate on time, taking possession and responsibility but not receiving a deed, is a(n)
   a. option agreement.
   b. land contract.
   c. contingency agreement.
   d. memorandum of sale.

5. The state law that requires deeds, real estate sales contracts, and certain leases to be in writing to be legally enforceable is the
   a. statute of limitations.
   b. statute of frauds.
   c. statute of contracts.
   d. New York Land Sales and Real Property Conveyances Law.

6. *Specific performance* refers to which of the following?
   a. A legal action to recover money damages resulting from a breach of contract.
   b. The ordinary compliance by the parties with the terms and conditions of a valid contract.
   c. One of the essential elements of a valid contract.
   d. A legal action to compel one party to comply with the terms and conditions of a valid contract.

7. All of the following are essential elements of a valid contract, *EXCEPT*
   a. acceptance.
   b. signature of the parties.
   c. legality of object.
   d. monetary consideration.

8. A contract that appears to be valid, but with which a party cannot be forced to comply is what type of contract?
   a. Unilateral   c. Unenforceable
   b. Invalid   d. Equitable

9. A contract that has no legal force or effect because it lacks one of the essential elements is referred to as what type of contract?
   a. Void   c. Unenforceable
   b. Voidable   d. Unilateral

10. A contract that, while valid, may be legally disaffirmed or rejected by one of the parties is referred to as what type of contract?
    a. Void   c. Unenforceable
    b. Voidable   d. Unilateral

CHAPTER NINE

TITLE CLOSING AND COSTS

■ TOPIC REVIEW

What is the difference between actual notice and constructive notice?

■ *Actual notice* refers to real knowledge: information obtained by firsthand observation or investigation.

■ *Constructive notice* of interests in or ownership of real estate is given to the world by the act of recording in the public records.

■ *Possession* of real estate gives constructive notice of the possible rights of the possessor.

What forms of title evidence are used in New York and elsewhere?

■ Abstract of title and lawyer's opinion
■ Owner's title insurance policy
■ Torrens certificate
■ Certificate of title

Does a deed constitute proof of title?

■ A deed does not prove that the grantor has any actual interest in the property being conveyed. It only proves that a prior grantor transferred his or her interest.

What are the characteristics of homeowner's insurance policies?

■ A standard policy protects a homeowner against losses from fire, theft, and liability. It may also be extended to cover other risks.

■ A coinsurance clause in a homeowner's policy requires the policyholder to insure for at least 80 percent of the property's replacement cost.

■ Insurance policies that cover only personal property are available to people who live in apartments and condominiums.

- For property located in or near a flood plain, flood insurance is required in order to obtain a federally-related mortgage loan.

What is RESPA?

- RESPA is a federal law: the *Real Estate Settlement Procedures Act.*
- RESPA requires that all settlement costs be disclosed when financing for the purchase of residential real estate is obtained through a federally-related loan.
- RESPA requires lenders to use a Uniform Settlement statement that includes the mandatory financial disclosures.

What is the purpose of a closing statement?

- A closing statement shows the actual amount paid and received by the parties at closing.
- The statement lists the sales price and earnest money deposit, and reflects any adjustments and prorations.

■ KEY TERMS GLOSSARY

abstract of title The condensed history of the title to a particular parcel of real estate.

accrued item On a closing statement, items of expense that have been incurred but are not yet payable, such as interest on a mortgage loan.

actual notice Knowledge obtained through first-hand observation or experience.

adjustments Divisions of financial responsibility between a buyer and seller (also called prorations).

affidavit A written statement sworn to before an authorized officer.

attorney's opinion of title Report in which a lawyer examines and evaluates an abstract of title.

caveat emptor A Latin phrase, meaning Let the buyer beware.

chain of title The conveyance of real property to one owner from another, reaching back to the original grantor.

coinsurance clause A clause in an insurance policy covering real property that requires the policyholder to maintain fire insurance coverage generally equal to at least 80 percent of the property's actual replacement cost.

constructive notice Notice given to the world by recorded documents. Possession of property is also considered constructive notice.

credit On a closing statement, an amount entered in a person's favor; an amount that has been paid or which must be reimbursed.

debit On a closing statement, a charge or amount a party owes and must pay at the closing.

escrow The closing of a transaction through a third party (escrow agent); also a special account for earnest money deposits or a mortgagee's trust account for insurance and tax payments.

evidence of title Proof of ownership of property; commonly a certificate of title, a title insurance policy, an abstract of title with a lawyer's opinion or Torrens certificate.

homeowner's insurance policy A standardized package insurance policy that covers a residential real estate owner against financial loss from fire, theft, public liability, and other commercial risks.

liability coverage Standard package homeowner's insurance policy coverage for personal injuries to others resulting from the insured's acts or negligence, voluntary medical payments and funeral expenses for accidents sustained by guests or resident employees on the property and physical damage to others' property.

marketable title Good or clear title reasonably free from the risk of litigation over defects.

mortgage reduction certificate Instrument executed by a mortgagee setting forth the present status and the balance due on the mortgage as of the date of the execution of the instrument.

prepaid item On a closing statement, an item to be prorated (such as fuel oil left in a tank) that has been paid for by the seller but not fully used up; a credit to the seller.

proration An expense, either prepaid or paid in arrears, that is divided or distributed between buyer and seller at the closing.

public records Records maintained by the recorder of deeds, registrar, county clerk, county treasurer, city clerk or clerks of various courts, and records involving taxes, special assessments, and other similar issues that are open for inspection by the public.

Real Estate Settlement Procedures Act (RESPA) The federal law that requires certain disclosures to consumers about mortgage loan settlements. RESPA also prohibits paying or receiving kickbacks and certain referral fees.

reconciliation The final step in the appraisal process, in which the appraiser combines the estimates of value received from the sales comparison, cost, and income approaches to arrive at a final estimate of market value for the subject property.

replacement cost The construction cost at current prices of a property that is not necessarily an exact duplicate of the subject property, but that serves the same purpose or function as the original.

suit to quiet title A court action intended to establish or settle the title to a property, especially when there is a cloud on the title.

survey The process by which boundaries are measured and land areas are determined; the on-sit measurement of lot lines, dimensions and position of a house on a lot, including the determination of any existing encroachments or easements.

title insurance policy A policy insuring the owner or mortgagee against loss by reason of defects in the title to a parcel of real estate, other than the encumbrances, defects, and matters specifically excluded by the policy.

title search The examination of public records relating to real estate to determine the current state of the ownership.

Torrens system A method of evidencing title by registration with the proper public authority, generally called the registrar.

Uniform Settlement Statement (HUD Form 1) A special form designed to detail all financial particulars of a transaction.

■ PASS-POINT CHECKLIST

■ Public Records and Recording

- ■ Recording Acts
- ■ Necessity for Recording
- ■ Notice
- ■ Chain of Title

■ Evidence of Title

- ■ Abstract of Title and Lawyer's Opinion
- ■ Title Insurance
- ■ The Torrens System
- ■ Certificate of Title
- ■ Marketable Title

■ Closing the Transaction

- ■ Where Closings Are Held and Who Attends
- ■ Broker's Role at Closing
- ■ Lender's Interest in Closing
- ■ Homeowners' Insurance
- ■ Federal Flood Insurance Program
- ■ RESPA Requirements

■ The Title Procedure

- ■ Checking the Premises
- ■ Releasing Existing Liens

■ Closing in Escrow

■ Preparation of Closing Statements

- ■ How the Closing Statement Works
- ■ Expenses
- ■ Prorations
- ■ Accounting for Credits and Charges

■ The Arithmetic of Proration

- ■ Prorations

■ PRACTICE QUESTIONS

1. A prospective buyer would have actual notice of the fact that a property was currently occupied if
   a. the current owner had properly recorded title in the county in which the property was located.
   b. the buyer visited the property and saw the occupants living there.
   c. the occupants currently possessed the property.
   d. the current owner's mortgage was properly recorded with the county clerk.

2. Which of the following is *not* evidence of title?
   a. Torrens certificate
   b. Abstract of title and lawyer's opinion
   c. HUD Form 1
   d. Certificate of title

3. A coinsurance clause requires insurance for what percentage of a property's replacement cost?
   a. 50   c. 70
   b. 60   d. 80

4. The condensed history of the title to a particular parcel of real estate is referred to as a(n)
   a. abstract of title.
   b. chain of title.
   c. attorney's opinion of title.
   d. public record of title.

5. Recording documents in the public record gives what type of notice to the world?
   a. Actual   c. Public
   b. Constructive d. Possessory

6. An amount that has been previously paid or which must be reimbursed to the party is entered on the closing statement as a(n)
   a. credit.   c. liability.
   b. debit.   d. escrow.

7. A prepaid expense divided or distributed between the buyer and seller at closing is a(n)
   a. credit.   c. liability.
   b. debit.   d. proration.

8. Certain disclosures about mortgage loan costs are required to be provided to consumers by
   a. the Torrens System.
   b. the Uniform Settlement Statement.
   c. RESPA.
   d. the doctrine of *caveat emptor.*

9. A closing statement
   a. proves that the grantor has transferred his or her interest in the property being sold.
   b. gives constructive notice to the world.
   c. is a tool to compute the actual amount to be paid by the buyer at closing.
   d. is the equivalent of an abstract of title.

10. On a closing statement, a charge or amount a party owes and must pay is reflected as a(n)
    a. credit.   c. adjustment.
    b. debit.   d. accrued item.

10

MORTGAGES

■ TOPIC REVIEW

Who are the parties to a mortgage?

■ The borrower (mortgagor)
■ The lender (mortgagee)

How does a mortgage work, in general?

■ First, the mortgagor (borrower) executes a *note* in which he or she agrees to repay the debt.
■ The note sets the rate of interest the borrower must pay as a charge for borrowing the money, or *principal.*
■ The note provides for amortization, the repayment schedule (term) of principal and interest.
■ The mortgagor also executes a *mortgage*, which places a lien on the property as security for the note.
■ The mortgage document is recorded, giving notice of the lender's interest and rights.
■ When the mortgage has been paid in full, the borrower is entitled to a satisfaction (release), which is also recorded. Recording the release clears the mortgage lien.

What happens if the borrower defaults?

■ If a borrower defaults, the lender may accelerate the payments, and a foreclosure sale may result.
■ If the proceeds of the foreclosure sale are insufficient to satisfy the debt, the lender may seek a deficiency judgment.

Are subsequent owners liable for an outstanding deficiency judgment?

■ A subsequent owner is personally liable for a deficiency judgment if he or she *assumes* the loan.

■ A subsequent owner who acquires the property *subject to* the mortgage is not liable for a deficiency judgment against the previous owner.

What is usury?

■ Usury is the illegal practice of charging more than the maximum interest rate permitted by New York law. The usury ceiling in New York floats: it is adjusted periodically by the State Banking Board.

■ Sellers who take back mortgages (called "seller financing"), loans to corporations, and loans greater than $2.5 million are exempt from the statutory usury ceiling.

What is a point?

■ A point is an up-front fee charged by the lender.

■ One point is equal to 1 percent of the new loan.

■ KEY TERMS GLOSSARY

acceleration clause The clause in a note or mortgage that can be enforced to make the entire debt due immediately if the mortgagor defaults.

adjustable-rate mortgage (ARM) A mortgage loan in which the interest rate may increase or decrease to specific intervals, following an economic indicator.

alienation clause The clause in a mortgage stating that the balance of the secured debt becomes immediately due and payable at the mortgagee's option if the property is sold.

amortized loan A loan in which the principal as well as the interest is payable in monthly or other periodic installments over the term of the loan.

annual percentage rate (APR) Rate of interest charged on a loan, calculated to take into account up-front loan fees and points. Usually higher than the contract interest rate.

assuming a mortgage Acquiring title to property on which there is an existing mortgage and agreeing to be personally liable for the terms and conditions of the mortgage, including payment.

balloon payment The final payment of a mortgage loan that is considerably larger than the required periodic payments because the loan amount was not fully amortized.

biweekly mortgage A loan that is paid in 26 half-month (biweekly) payments each year, resulting in an earlier payoff and lower interest costs over the life of the loan.

bond The evidence of a personal debt secured by a mortgage or other lien on real estate.

buydown A financing technique used to reduce the monthly payments for the first few years of a loan. Funds in the form of discount points are given to the lender by the builder or seller to buy down or lower the effective interest rate paid by the buyer, thus reducing the monthly payments for a set time.

default The nonperformance of a duty, whether arising under a contract or otherwise; failure to meet an obligation when due.

deficiency judgment A personal judgment levied against the mortgagor when a foreclosure sale does not produce sufficient funds to pay the mortgage debt in full.

down payment The amount of cash that a purchaser will pay at closing.

equity The interest or value that an owner has in property over and above any mortgage indebtedness and other liens.

estoppel certificate A document in which a borrower certifies the amount he or she owes on a mortgage loan and the rate of interest (similar to a *reduction certificate*).

foreclosure A procedure whereby property pledged as security for a debt is sold to pay the debt in the event of default in payments or terms.

grace period Time allowed beyond a specified performance or payment date before a default occurs.

interest A charge made by a lender for the use of money.

lien theory Some states interpret a mortgage as being purely a lien on real property. The mortgagee has no right of possession but must foreclose the lien and sell the property if the mortgagor defaults. New York is a lien theory state.

loan servicing The lender's duties in administering a loan, such as collecting payments, accounting and bookkeeping, maintaining records and issuing loan status reports to the borrower.

loan-to-value (LTV) ratio The relationship between the amount of the mortgage loan and the value of the real estate being pledged as collateral.

mortgage bankers Companies that are licensed to make real estate loans that are sold to investors.

mortgage broker An individual who acts as an intermediary between lenders and borrowers for a fee.

mortgagee A lender in a mortgage loan transaction.

mortgagor A borrower who conveys his or her property as security for a loan.

note An instrument of credit given to attest a debt.

PITI Principal, interest, taxes, and insurance: components of a regular mortgage payment.

points A unit of measurement used for various loan charges; one point equals 1 percent of the amount of the loan.

prepayment (penalty) A charge imposed on a borrower who pays off the loan principal early.

primary mortgage market Lenders who make loans directly to real estate borrowers.

principal The amount borrowed on which interest is paid.

private mortgage insurance (PMI) Insurance provided by private carrier that protects a lender against a loss in the event of a foreclosure and deficiency.

purchase-money mortgage (PMM) A note secured by a mortgage or deed of trust given by a buyer, as borrower, to a seller, as lender, as part of the purchase price of the real estate.

reduction certificate A statement from the lender detailing the amount remaining and currently due on a mortgage, usually sought when a mortgage is being assumed or prepaid (also referred to as an *estoppel certificate*).

satisfaction of mortgage A document acknowledging the payment of a debt.

Sonny Mae (SONYMA) The State of New York Mortgage Agency.

straight (term) loan A loan in which only interest is paid during the term of the loan, with the entire principal amount due with the final interest payment.

subject to a mortgage When property is taken "subject to" a mortgage, the purchaser is not personally liable to the mortgagee for satisfaction of the pre-existing debt (unless he or she agrees to be held liable).

term The originally scheduled period of time over which a loan is to be paid.

usury Charging interest at a rate higher than the maximum established by law.

■ PASS-POINT CHECKLIST

- ■ **Definition of Mortgage**
  - ■ Loan Instruments
  - ■ Duties of the Mortgagor
  - ■ Provisions for Default
  - ■ Foreclosure
  - ■ Sale of Property That is Mortgaged
  - ■ Recording of the Mortgage
  - ■ Satisfaction of the Mortgage Lien

- ■ **Types of Mortgages**
  - ■ Primary Sources of Real Estate Financing

- ■ **Payment Plans**
  - ■ Types of Amortization
  - ■ Interest
  - ■ Tax-Deductible Interest Payments
  - ■ Prepayment
  - ■ Tax and Insurance Reserves

■ PRACTICE QUESTIONS

1. In a typical mortgage relationship, the *mortgagor* is the
   a. lender.
   b. previous owner.
   c. borrower.
   d. title insurer.

2. In a typical mortgage relationship, the *mortgagee* is the
   a. lender.   c. borrower.
   b. previous owner.   d. title insurer.

3. Which of the following clears a mortgage lien?
   a. Payment of the mortgage in full
   b. Recording the note and mortgage
   c. Issuance of a release (satisfaction)
   d. Recording the release

4. What is the statutory usury ceiling in New York?
   a. 10 percent
   b. 20 percent
   c. It is adjusted periodically
   d. There is none

5. All of the following transactions would be exempt from New York's usury law, *EXCEPT* a
   a. seller-financed sale.
   b. loan made to a corporation.
   c. $3 million loan.
   d. $2.5 million loan.

6. What is a *point*?
   a. An up-front fee charged by the lender, equal to 1 percent of the sales price of the property
   b. An up-front fee charged by the lender, equal to 1 percent of the loan amount
   c. An up-front fee charged by the lender, equal to 1 percent of the annualized interest rate
   d. The prorated equivalent value of the ownership in the property aside from the mortgage

7. In which case would a subsequent owner be held personally liable for a deficiency judgment against the original borrower?
   a. If the subsequent owner assumed the loan
   b. If the subsequent owner acquired the property subject to the mortgage
   c. If the subsequent owner acquired the property in a seller-financed transaction
   d. If the proceeds of the foreclosure sale are insufficient to satisfy the debt

8. A mortgage in which the interest rate may be increased or decreased at certain intervals depending on the behavior of a specific economic indicator is a(n)
   a. ARM.   c. balloon loan.
   b. term loan.   d. amortized loan.

9. New York follows which mortgage theory?
   a. Lien   c. Equity
   b. Estoppel   d. Title

10. The relationship between the amount of a mortgage loan and the value of the real estate being pledged as collateral is known as its
    a. PITI ratio.   c. APR.
    b. LTV ratio.   d. buydown.

11

REAL ESTATE FINANCE I

■ TOPIC REVIEW

What are the types of mortgage loans available to home buyers?

■ Typical mortgage loans include conventional loans, FHA-insured loans, and VA-guaranteed loans. Other loans are available from private lenders. Private mortgage insurers may insure mortgages as well.

What are some of the special rules that apply to FHA and VA loans?

■ Lenders are permitted to charge reasonable discount points. (Each discount point is equivalent to 1 percent of the loan.)
■ FHA and VA mortgages may be assumed, although certain exceptions apply and strict regulations must be complied with.

What are some of the ways in which a mortgage loan may be structured?

■ Purchase-money mortgage
■ Buydown
■ Graduated-payment loan
■ Shared-equity loan
■ Reverse annuity mortgage
■ Blanket mortgage
■ Package mortgage
■ Open-end mortgage
■ Wraparound mortgage
■ Construction loan
■ Sale-and-leaseback agreement
■ Land contract
■ Investment group financing

How does an adjustable-rate mortgage work?

■ In an adjustable-rate mortgage, the interest rate is raised or lowered each adjustment period to reflect the behavior of a particular mortgage rate index.

■ The adjusted rate includes a margin, or an amount added to the index rate to cover the lender's costs of doing business. The margin generally remains the same through the life of the loan.

What is meant by negative amortization?

■ Negative amortization refers to a situation in which the monthly payments on a loan fail to cover the interest payment due.

■ The result of negative amortization is that the total debt increases rather than decreasing as in normal amortization.

What is the secondary mortgage market?

■ The secondary mortgage market is made up of investors who purchase mortgage loans to hold as investments.

Who are the federally-related participants in the secondary mortgage market?

■ FNMA, the Federal National Mortgage Association (Fannie Mae)
■ GNMA, Government National Mortgage Association (Ginnie Mae)
■ FHLMC, the Federal Home Loan Mortgage Corporation (Freddie Mac)
■ FNMA, GNMA, and FHLMC purchase loans from the originators and hold them (warehousing) until investors are available to purchase them.

What is Regulation Z?

■ Regulation Z is a federal law, also known as the Truth-in-Lending Law.
■ It requires that institutional lenders disclose all finance charges to borrowers.
■ A lender's failure to comply with the disclosure requirements can result in severe penalties.

What are a lender's main concerns in underwriting a loan?

■ Does the borrower's income debt and employment history suggest the likelihood that he or she will repay the debt according to its terms?
■ Is the value of the property sufficient to cover the mortgage in the event that the borrower defaults and the property is sold at a foreclosure sale?

How does a lender evaluate the sufficiency of a borrower's income?

■ Two ratios are usually applied: (1) the borrower may not spend more than a specific percentage of his or her gross monthly income on housing expenses (28 percent is typical); and (2) the borrower may not spend more than a specific percentage of his or her gross monthly income on housing expenses and other long-term debt payments combined (typically 36 percent).

■ KEY TERMS GLOSSARY

blanket mortgage A mortgage covering more than one parcel of real estate, providing for each parcel's partial release from the mortgage lien upon repayment of a definite portion of the debt.

bridge loan A short-term loan designed to cover a gap between the sale of one property and the purchase of another (also called a *swing loan, temporary loan,* or *interim financing*).

cap A limit on how much the interest rate or payment might be raised in each period of an ARM.

ceiling A limit beyond which the interest rate or monthly payment on a loan may not increase.

construction loan See *interim financing.*

conventional loan A loan that requires no insurance or guarantee.

convertibility An adjustable-rate mortgage in which the borrower may elect to change to a fixed-rate mortgage, either whenever current rates are favorable, or at specific set conversion dates.

ECOA (Equal Credit Opportunity Act) The federal law that prohibits discrimination in the extension of credit because of race, color, religion, national origin, sex, age, or marital status.

Fannie Mae (FNMA) A quasi-governmental agency established to purchase any kind of mortgage loans in the secondary mortgage market from the primary lenders.

FHA loan A loan insured by the Federal Housing Administration and made by an approved lender in a accordance with the FHA's regulations.

Freddie Mac (FHLMC) A corporation established to purchase primarily conventional mortgage loans in the secondary mortgage market.

Ginnie Mae (GNMA) A government agency that plays an important role in the secondary mortgage market. It sells mortgage-backed securities that are backed by pools of FHA and VA loans.

home equity loan A loan (sometimes called a *line of credit*) under which a property owner uses his or her residence as collateral and can the withdraw funds up to a prearranged amount against the property.

imputed interest An IRS concept that treats some concessionary low-interest loans as if they had been paid and collected at a statutory rate.

index With an adjustable-rate mortgage, a measure of current interest rates; a basis for calculating the new rate at the time of adjustment.

interim financing A short-term loan usually made during the construction phase of a building project (in this case often referred to as a *construction loan*).

jumbo loan A loan that exceeds FNMA and FHLMC maximum loan limit.

margin With an adjustable-rate mortgage, the number of points over an *index* at which the interest rate is set.

mortgage insurance premium (MIP) Lump sum premium for mortgage insurance coverage, payable either in cash at closing or financed over the mortgage term.

negative amortization Gradual building up of a large mortgage debt when payments are not sufficient to cover interest due and reduce the principal.

nonconforming mortgage A flexible loan that does not satisfy standard uniform underwriting requirements.

open-end mortgage A mortgage loan that is expandable by increments up to a maximum dollar amount, the full loan being secured by the same original mortgage.

package loan A real estate loan used to finance the purchase of both real property and personal property, such as in the purchase of a new home that includes carpeting, window coverings, and major appliances.

RESPA statement The Real Estate Settlement Act requirement that lenders inform both buyers and sellers in advance of all fees for the settlement of a residential mortgage loan.

Regulation Z Implements the Truth-in-Lending Act requiring credit institutions to inform borrowers of the true cost of obtaining credit.

release clause A clause in a mortgage under which part of a mortgaged property may be released from a lien.

reverse-annuity mortgage A loan under which the homeowner receives monthly payments based on his or her accumulated equity rather than a lump sum. The loan must be repaid at a prearranged date or upon the death of the owner or the sale of the property.

sale-and-leaseback A transaction in which an owner sells his or her improved property and, as part of the same transaction, signs a long-term lease to remain in possession of the premises.

secondary mortgage market A market for the purchase and sale of existing mortgages, designed to provide greater liquidity for mortgages; also called the *secondary money market*. Mortgages are first originated in the *primary mortgage market*.

shared-equity mortgage Loan in which the purchaser receives assistance (such as help with the down payment, a reduced interest rate, or help with monthly payments) from a partner (such as a lender, relative, or the seller), who receives a share of the profit when the property is eventually sold.

swing loan A short term loan similar to a *bridge loan* that uses the strength of the borrower's equity in the property he or she is selling, to purchase a new property.

underwriting The process by which a lender evaluates a prospective borrower's application through verification of employment and financial information and analysis of credit and appraisal reports.

VA loan A mortgage loan on approved property made to a qualified veteran by an authorized lender and guaranteed by the Department of Veterans Affairs in order to limit the lender's possible loss.

wraparound mortgage A method of refinancing in which the new mortgage is placed in a secondary, or subordinate, position; the new mortgage includes both the unpaid principal balance of the first mortgage and whatever additional sums are advanced by the lender. In essence is an additional mortgage in which another lender refinances a borrower by lending an amount over the existing first mortgage amount without disturbing the existence of the first mortgage.

■ PASS-POINT CHECKLIST

- ■ **Types of Loans**
  - ■ Private Mortgages

- ■ **Methods of Finance**
  - ■ Conventional Loans
  - ■ FHA-Insured Loans
  - ■ VA-Guaranteed Loans
  - ■ Government Backing via the Secondary Market

- ■ **Financing Legislation**
  - ■ Regulation Z
  - ■ Federal Equal Credit Opportunity Act

- ■ **Lender's Criteria for Granting a Loan**
  - ■ Evaluating the Property
  - ■ Evaluating the Potential Borrower

■ PRACTICE QUESTIONS

1. The limit on the size of any single interest rate adjustment in an ARM is referred to as the
   a. margin.
   b. ceiling.
   c. cap.
   d. ratio.

2. The maximum range of rate adjustments permitted over the life of a loan is called a
   a. margin.
   b. ceiling.
   c. cap.
   d. ratio.

3. The amount added to an adjustable-rate mortgage's index rate to cover the lender's costs is called a
   a. margin.
   b. ceiling.
   c. cap.
   d. ratio.

4. All of the following are federally-related participants in the secondary mortgage market, *EXCEPT*
   a. FNMA.
   b. GNMA.
   c. ECOA.
   d. FHLMC.

5. Which federal law is also known as the "Truth in Lending" Act?
   a. ECOA
   b. RESPA
   c. Fair Housing Act
   d. Regulation Z

6. A short-term loan designed to cover a gap between the sale of one property and the purchase of another is a
   a. participation loan.
   b. wraparound mortgage.
   c. bridge loan.
   d. takeout loan.

7. What is Fannie Mae?
   a. A corporation established to purchase primarily conventional mortgage loans in the secondary market
   b. A quasi-government agency established to purchase mortgage loans in the secondary market from primary lenders
   c. A government agency that sells mortgage-backed securities backed by pools of FHA and VA loans
   d. A government agency that insures certain qualified loans made by lenders approved under its regulations

8. Which of the following loans is used primarily in new construction projects?
   a. Swing   c. Takeout
   b. Wraparound   d. Package

9. The gradual building-up of a large mortgage debt when payments do not cover interest or reduce the principal amount is a characteristic of
   a. disintermediation.
   b. convertibility.
   c. imputed interest.
   d. negative amortization.

10. A transaction in which an owner sells his or her improved property and, as part of the same transaction, signs a long-term lease to remain in possession of the premises is a(n)
    a. reverse-annuity loan.
    b. participation agreement.
    c. equity-sharing agreement.
    d. sale and leaseback agreement.

12

LAND-USE REGULATIONS

■ TOPIC REVIEW

What is the difference between a private and a public land-use control?

- *Private land-use controls* are the way owners (frequently subdividers) maintain the character or control the use of subdivision lots.
- Private land-use controls are exercised through the use of deed restrictions applicable to all lots. The restrictions are recorded, and may be enforced by adjacent lot owners through a court injunction to correct a violation of the restriction.
- *Public land-use controls* arise from the state's police power to protect the public health, safety, and welfare.
- The state's *police powers* are exercised through ordinances and statutes. Other governing bodies, such as cities and municipalities, enforce public land-use controls through the use of master plans and zoning ordinances.

What are the government's powers over the use and ownership of land by private individuals?

- Certain government powers impose limits on private land rights: taxation, eminent domain, police power, and escheat. Public ownership ensures the availability of land for necessary public purposes, such as parks, roads, and schools.
- State and federal government agencies are empowered to preserve natural resources through environmental legislation and controls, such as CERCLA and SARA, and wetlands legislation.
- CERCLA and SARA make landowners responsible for environmental cleanups.

What are zoning ordinances?

- A zoning ordinance is a legal device used by municipalities to control development by separating residential neighborhoods from commercial and industrial uses.
- Zoning is used to control land use, building height and bulk, development, and population density.

Is there any way around a zoning ordinance?

- Zoning boards of appeal are established to consider applications for (and to grant or deny) special-use permits, variances, and to allow nonconforming uses.

What is a building code?

- Building codes are local ordinances that control the quality of new and existing construction by setting specific standards for foundations, structural elements, and internal systems such as plumbing, sewers, wiring, and ventilation.
- Building codes are enforced through permits and periodic site and plan inspections.
- When a new building meets local standards, the building inspector may issue a certificate of occupancy that permits the structure to be used.

■ KEY TERMS GLOSSARY

abutting Two parcels of real estate (or anything else) immediately next to each other.

accessory apartment uses A small additional apartment that is sometimes permitted in an area otherwise zoned for single-family homes, possibly used for a small home business or elderly relative.

ad valorem tax A tax levied according to value, generally used to refer to real estate tax. Also called the *general tax*.

assessed value A valuation placed on property as a basis for taxation.

building codes Regulations established by state and local governments fully stating the structural requirements for building.

building permit Written permission from the local government to build or alter a structure.

census tract A geographic area defined by the Bureau of the Census.

CERCLA (Comprehensive Environmental Response Compensation and Liability Act) Enacted in 1980 and reauthorized by the Super-fund Amendments and Reauthorization Act of 1986 (SARA), this federal law imposes liability on lenders, occupants, operators, and owners for correcting environmental problems discovered on a property.

certificate of occupancy (C of O) Document issued by a municipal authority stating that a building complies with building, health, and safety codes and may be occupied.

cluster zoning Zoning that permits buildings to be grouped on small lots, allowing extra open space.

condemnation A judicial or administrative proceeding to exercise the power of eminent domain through which a government agency takes private property for public use and compensates the owner.

deed restriction An imposed restriction in a deed for the purpose of limiting the use of the land by future owners.

demography The study of population statistics.

direct public ownership Land-use control method through which land is owned by the government for such public uses as municipal buildings, parks, schools, and roads.

doctrine of laches Loss of a legal right through undue delay in asserting it. Commonly known as the statute of limitations.

eminent domain The right of a government or quasi-public body to acquire property for public use through a court action called *condemnation*.

escheat The reversion of property to the state or county, as provided by state law, in cases where a person dies intestate without heirs capable of inheriting or when the property is abandoned.

group home A living unit in which more than three unrelated individuals reside.

home occupations Small business or other activities in which residents in otherwise residentially-zoned areas are permitted to engage.

infrastructure Public works, such as utilities, roads, sewers, etc.

lead agency The agency that coordinates an environmental survey.

master plan A comprehensive plan to guide the long-term physical development of a particular area.

moratorium In real estate, temporary halt to development in a community.

nonconforming use A use of property that is permitted to continue after a zoning ordinance prohibiting it has been established for the area.

OPRHP Office of Parks, Recreation, and Historic Preservation.

police power The government's right to impose laws, statutes, and ordinances, including zoning ordinances and building codes, to protect the public health, safety and welfare.

restrictive covenant A clause in a deed that limits the way real estate ownership may be used.

SARA (Superfund Amendments and Reauthorization Act) Federal law defining landowner responsibility for cleanup of environmental contamination resulting from past activities. Establishes innocent landowner defense against liability for contamination cause by prior owners.

setbacks The distance required by a local zoning regulation between a lot line and a building.

special assessments A tax or levy customarily imposed against only those specific parcels of real estate that will benefit from a proposed public improvement like a street or sewer.

special-use permit Permission granted by a local government to allow a use of property that, although in conflict with zoning regulations, is nonetheless in the public interest (a house of worship in a residential neighborhood, for instance, or a restaurant in an industrial zone).

spot zoning Special zoning actions that affect only a small area. Uses that are not in harmony with the surrounding uses are illegal in New York.

subdivision regulations Municipal ordinances that establish requirement for subdivisions and developments.

taking A government restriction on the use of an owner's property for which the owner must be compensated.

taxation The process by which a government or municipal quasi-public body raises monies to fund its operation.

transfer of development rights A means by which a developer can purchase a landowner's property rights.

variance Permission obtained from zoning authorities to build a structure or conduct a use that is expressly prohibited by the current zoning laws; an exception from the zoning ordinances.

zoning boards of appeal Official local government bodies established to hear complaints about the impact of zoning ordinances on individual properties, and to consider variances and special-use permits.

zoning ordinances An exercise of police power by a municipality to regulate and control the character and use of property.

■ PASS-POINT CHECKLIST

- ■ **Planning for the Future**
- ■ **Private Land-Use Controls**
  - ■ Enforcement of Deed Restrictions

- ■ **Government Powers**
  - ■ Taxation

- ■ **Government Land-Use Controls**

- ■ **Public Land-Use Controls**
  - ■ The Mast Plan
  - ■ Zoning
  - ■ Building Codes
  - ■ Subdivision Regulations

■ Development Rights
■ Environmental Protection Legislation
■ Landmark Preservation
■ Direct Public Ownership

■ PRACTICE QUESTIONS

1. A developer who wanted to ensure that no homes in a subdivision would ever have a garden shed or doghouse in the backyard could do so by
   a. exercising his or her power of eminent domain.
   b. recording a deed restriction.
   c. enforcing the subdivision's master plan.
   d. obtaining a court injunction.

2. Taxation and escheat are examples of
   a. private land-use controls.
   b. government police powers.
   c. public land-use controls.
   d. zoning powers.

3. Which of the following would most likely regulate the type of electrical wiring allowed in a proposed new building?
   a. Zoning ordinances
   b. Building codes
   c. Deed restrictions
   d. Eminent domain

4. A legal device used by municipalities to control development by separating various land uses is a
   a. zoning ordinance.
   b. deed restriction.
   c. variance.
   d. building code.

5. All the following are devices for avoiding strict compliance with a zoning ordinance, *EXCEPT*
   a. special-use permits.
   b. permissible nonconforming uses.
   c. variances.
   d. escheat.

6. A document issued by a municipal authority stating that a building complies with certain quality standards is a(n)
   a. building permit.
   b. special-use permit.
   c. certificate of occupancy.
   d. special assessment.

7. The power of eminent domain is exercised through
   a. a certiorari proceeding.
   b. a condemnation suit.
   c. escheat.
   d. zoning ordinances.

8. A zoning board's decision to zone a 500-square-foot area in the middle of a residential neighborhood for heavy industry in order to allow the construction of an explosives factory would be an example of
   a. illegal spot zoning.
   b. a special-use permit.
   c. a nonconforming use.
   d. legal eminent domain.

9. The government's right to impose laws, statutes, and ordinances to protect the public health, safety, and welfare is referred to as
   a. police power.
   b. condemnation.
   c. eminent domain.
   d. escheat.

10. A use of property permitted even after a change in the local zoning ordinance prohibits such uses is referred to as a(n)
    a. special-use permit.
    b. nonconforming use.
    c. special assessment.
    d. variance.

13

INTRODUCTION TO CONSTRUCTION

■ TOPIC REVIEW

What are the parts of a foundation?

■ Foundations are composed of footings, foundation walls, and slabs.

■ Concrete slab and pier-and-beam are the two most common types of foundation.

What is the most common type of construction in the state of New York?

■ Wood-frame construction is the most common type of construction for single-family houses in this state.

What are three types of exterior wall framing?

■ *Platform framing*: floors are constructed consecutively, one at a time, with each floor serving as a platform for the next story. Also called western frame construction.

■ *Balloon*: wall studs extend from the floor of the first floor continuously to the top of the second floor, rather than being attached one floor at a time. Provides an even, unbroken exterior wall surface largely immune from the shifting effects of settling.

■ *Post-and-beam*: uses interior posts to support ceiling planks and upper floors. Offers more potential for open floor space.

What are the different styles of windows?

■ *Sash*: vertically sliding single- or double-hung construction, stabilized by the interaction of weights and pulleys

■ *Slider*: horizontally sliding sash

■ *Casement*: may be hinged on the side or opened vertically, in either case operated by a gear assembly

■ *Jalousie*: horizontal slats of glass opened and closed by a mechanical system of gears and hinges

What are some different styles of doors?

■ *Panel*: interior or exterior door made of solid wood or plywood with raised or flat decorative panels (some panels are often glass in exterior panel doors)
■ *Slab*: (also called solid core flush doors) interior or exterior doors, flat on both sides, often with a veneer
■ *Hollow core*: interior doors with solid edges and a hollow or light-framed interior

What is skeleton roof framing?

■ A "skeleton" of roof rafters or upper chords covered with a plywood sheath and shingles made of fiberglass, wood, or asphalt
■ Types of skeleton roof framing include exposed rafter, joist and rafter, and truss.

How is a home's interior finished?

■ Drywall panels are affixed to interior wall frames and painted or wallpapered.
■ Wall finishings, decorative wood trim, floor coverings, and cabinets are installed last.

What are electrical systems?

■ Voltage indicates the strength of the electrical charge—most outlets are 110 volts.
■ Amperage indicates the amount of current that is flowing in response to the voltage. New York State code requires a minimum of 100 amps in all new construction.

How are building standards and construction quality determined?

■ Standards for health and safety in construction projects are established by local and state building codes. The quality of materials and construction for an individual project is determined by the working drawings and written specifications.

What are some of the laws and regulations governing home construction in New York?

■ New York state law regulates the sale of home improvement goods and services valued over $500 to homeowners or tenants.
■ Electrical, plumbing, heating, ventilation, and air conditioning systems must adhere to minimum state building codes as well as to more stringent local requirements.

What warranties are new home buyers entitled to by New York state law?

■ Defective construction and materials: 1 year

■ Defective electrical, plumbing, heating, ventilation, and air-conditioning systems: 2 years

■ Major structural defects: 6 years

■ KEY TERMS GLOSSARY

amperage The strength of an electrical current. New York State codes require a minimum of 100 amps in all new construction.

basement Space that is wholly or partly below grade.

beam A horizontal structural support member.

bearing walls Walls that physically support a ceiling, upper stories, or roof.

blueprint A plan for a building, including floor plan and specifications for the builder to follow.

British thermal unit (BTU) A unit of measure of heat, used to rate air conditioning and heating equipment capacity. One BTU raises one pound of water one degree Fahrenheit.

casement window Vertically or horizontally hinged window opened by crank system.

circuit breaker box Interior electrical distribution panel in homes containing circuit breaker switches rather than fuses.

concrete slab foundation Foundation made of poured concrete and steel rod reinforcement, resting on a waterproof sheet directly on the ground; supported by sunken concrete beams (footings).

crawlspace A basement or attic space that is too low for standing upright.

double-hung window Sash-style window with two vertical sashes.

eave A portion of a roof or other element that projects beyond the outside walls of a house.

fascia Board on the outside of a soffit.

flashing Material used to provide a waterproof seal on rooves, chimneys, and wall seams.

floating slab foundation Type of concrete slab foundation in which the footings and slab are poured separately.

foundation The main support for a house, composed of footings, foundation walls, columns, slab, and similar components.

framing The skeletal structure of a building.

girder A heavy wood or steel beam that provides structural support.

headers Horizontal support elements located above windows and doors.

heat pump Mechanism that uses heat from outside air to reduce heating and air-conditioning costs.

insulation Material placed between inner and outer surfaces to ensure protection against heat, cold, and moisture. Common insulating materials are fiberglass, Styrofoam, rock wool, and fiber (blown-in) insulation. The New York code sets regional insulation standards.

jalousie window Window style composed of narrow slats of glass that open or close by use of a system of gears and hinges.

joist and rafter roof Roofing system that relies on sloping timbers supported by a ridge board and made rigid by interconnecting joists.

Lally™ columns Vertical columns that support a building's main beams

110-volt circuit Standard residential electrical circuit, composed of one hot and one neutral wire, and a separate ground wire.

percolation rate How quickly liquid drains into the ground.

pier and beam foundation Foundation style in which partly-submerged columns (piers) support the foundation slab, with an air pocket (crawlspace) between the slab and the ground.

pitch The angle of a roof's slope determined by a ratio of height to span.

plaster board/wallboard Standard 4' by 8' panels often used instead of plaster as wall-finishing elements.

platform framing construction Common form of construction for one- and two-story residential buildings; one floor is built at a time, with the lower floor providing a platform on which the upper floor is built.

post and beam construction A framing method in which celing planks are set on beams.

R-value Numerical measurement of insulating material's resistance to heat transfer; a higher R-value indicates superior insulation.

septic system Individual residential wastewater treatment and disposal system.

sheathing Material applied to a building's frame to form walls.

siding The exterior wall finishing materials of a building.

sill plates Horizontal support elements found on top of a structure's foundation.

slab-on-grade construction A concrete slab poured on prepared earth to form a structure's foundation.

soffit Horizontal finishing element found on the underside of a roof overhang.

solar energy Use of solar collectors to convert heat from the sun into usable heat and energy for a building.

specifications An architect's or engineer's detailed instructions construction materials.

studs Vertical wall supports.

truss roof Particularly strong roofing system composed of chords, diagonals, and gusset plates, pre-assembled at a mill.

voltage Measurement of an electric current's force.

220-volt circuit Electrical circuit required by large appliances; composed of two hot wires, a neutral wire, and a ground wire.

■ PASS-POINT CHECKLIST

- ■ **Site Preparation**
- ■ **Regulation of Residential Construction**
- ■ **Wood-Frame Construction**
  - ■ Architectural Styles
  - ■ Foundations
- ■ **Exterior Construction**
  - ■ Walls and Framing
  - ■ Insulation
  - ■ Window and Door Units
  - ■ Roof Framing and Coverings
- ■ **Interior Construction**
  - ■ Walls and Finishing
  - ■ Plumbing
  - ■ Heating and Air-Conditioning
  - ■ Electrical Services
- ■ **New York Laws**
  - ■ Home Improvement Law
  - ■ New Home Warranty

■ PRACTICE QUESTIONS

1. All of the following are components of a foundation, *EXCEPT*
   - **a.** footings.
   - **b.** slab.
   - **c.** steel rods.
   - **d.** gussets.

2. The type of exterior wall framing in which wall studs extend all the way from the first floor to the second floor ceiling is
   - **a.** platform framing.
   - **b.** balloon framing.
   - **c.** post-and-beam framing.
   - **d.** truss framing.

3. A window that opens horizontally on a track is a
   - **a.** sash.
   - **b.** slider.
   - **c.** jalousie.
   - **d.** casement.

4. Two types of windows are opened and closed with gear systems. They are
   - **a.** sash and slider.
   - **b.** slider and jalousie.
   - **c.** jalousie and casement.
   - **d.** slider and casement.

5. Which of the following types of doors are used only on the interior of a house?
   a. Panel
   b. Slab
   c. Hollow core
   d. Solid core flush

6. What is the minimum value of home improvement goods and services to which the New York Home Improvement Law applies?
   a. $100
   b. $350
   c. $500
   d. $1,000

7. In New York, new home buyers are entitled to a warranty against defects in heating, ventilation, and electrical systems. How many years does this warranty last?
   a. One
   b. Two
   c. Three
   d. Six

8. In New York, new home buyers are entitled to a warranty against defects in construction and materials. How many years does this warranty last?
   a. One
   b. Two
   c. Three
   d. Six

9. In New York, new home buyers are entitled to a warranty against major structural defects. How many years does this warranty last?
   a. One
   b. Two
   c. Three
   d. Six

10. Which of the following R-values represents the most resistance to heat transfer?
    a. 0.95
    b. 1.50
    c. 8.00
    d. 3:AA

14

VALUATION PROCESS

What are land's economic characteristics?

- Scarcity
- Improvements
- Permanence of investment
- Area preference

What are land's physical characteristics?

- Immobility
- Nonhomogeneity
- Indestructibility

What is the difference between value and price?

- The *value* of a property is determined by how much its future benefits are worth today: the present worth of future benefits.
- The *price* of a property is determined by the marketplace.

What is market value?

- A property's *market value* is the price it will command in an open market, in a free and arm's-length transaction between a fully informed buyer and seller, neither of whom is under duress.

What is appraisal?

- To appraise real estate is to estimate its market value—the most probable sales price of the subject property.
- In New York, appraisers may be licensed or certified in four categories, depending on education and experience.

What are the three methods by which real property is appraised?

- *Cost approach*: estimates value based on how much it would cost to rebuild the structure being appraised, minus any loss due to physical, functional, or external depreciation.
- *Income capitalization approach*: estimates value based on the amount of income the property generates over time.
- *Direct sales comparison approach*: (also called the *market data approach*) estimates value by comparing it with similar properties that have sold.

What is GRM?

- The *gross rent multiplier* (GRM) is the sales price divided by gross monthly rent.

■ KEY TERMS GLOSSARY

amenities Elements that contribute to a property's attractiveness to owners and potential buyers.

appraisal An estimate of the quantity, quality, or value of something. The process through which conclusions of property value are obtained; also refers to the report that sets forth the process of estimation and conclusion of value.

Appraisal Institute A private, professional organization for appraisers.

arm's-length transaction A transaction between relative strangers, each trying to do the best for himself or herself.

assemblage The combining of two or more adjoining lots into one larger tract to increase their total value.

capitalization rate The rate of return a property will produce on the owner's investment.

CBS Memory aid for appraisers: Comparable Better, Subtract.

comparable property An appraisal term referring to a similar, nearby, recently sold property that can be analyzed in relation to the subject property.

comparative market analysis (CMA) A study, intended to assist an owner in establishing listing price, of recent comparable sales, properties that failed to sell and parcels presently on the market.

cost approach Process of estimating the value of property by adding to the estimated land value the appraiser's estimate of the reproduction or replacement cost of the building, less depreciation.

CPA Memory aid for appraisers: Comparable Poorer, Add.

demand The number of people who wish to purchase an available product at a specific price during a particular period of time.

depreciation In appraisal, a loss of value in property due to any cause including physical deterioration, functional obsolescence, and locational obsolescence.

direct sales comparison approach An appraisal method in which a subject property is evaluated in comparison with similar recently sold properties; most useful for single residential properties.

economic obsolescence Depreciation of a property due to economic factors; a form of external obsolescence.

external obsolescence Reduction in a property's value caused by factors outside the subject property, such as social or environmental forces or objectionable neighboring property.

fee appraiser An appraiser who works as an independent contractor.

functional obsolescence A loss of value to an improvement to real estate due to functional problems, often caused by age or poor design.

gross income multiplier A figure used as a multiplier of the gross annual income of a property to produce an estimate of the property's value.

gross rent multiplier The figure used as a multiplier of the gross monthly income of a property to produce an estimate of the property's value.

highest and best use The possible use of land that would produce the greatest net income and thereby develop the highest land value.

income capitalization approach The process of estimating the value of an income-producing property by capitalization of the annual net income expected to be produced by the property during its remaining useful life.

locational obsolescence A form of external obsolescence in which a property's value is reduced due to changes in the desirability of its location or changes beyond its property lines.

physical deterioration A reduction in a property's value resulting from a decline in physical condition; can be caused by action of the elements or by ordinary wear and tear.

plottage The increase in value or utility resulting from the consolidation (*assemblage*) of two or more adjacent lots into one larger lot.

progression An appraisal principle that states that, between dissimilar properties the value of the lesser-quality property is favorably affected by the presence of the better-quality property.

reconciliation The final step in the appraisal process, in which the appraiser combines the estimates of value received from the sales comparison, cost, and income approaches to arrive at a final estimate of market value for the subject property.

regression An appraisal principle that states that, between dissimilar properties, the value of the better-quality property is affected adversely by the presence of the lesser-quality property.

replacement cost The construction cost at current prices of a property that is not necessarily an exact duplicate of the subject property but serves the same purpose or function as the original.

reproduction cost The production cost at current prices of an exact duplicate of the subject property.

special-purpose buildings Real estate such as schools, hospitals, churches, and government-held land.

staff appraiser A professional in-house appraiser employed to perform appraisals on behalf of the employer.

subject property The property being appraised.

substitution An appraisal principle that states that the maximum value of a property tends to be set by the cost of purchasing an equally valuable and desirable substitute property, assuming that no costly delay is encountered in making the substitution.

supply The amount of goods available in the market to be sold at a given price. The term is often coupled with *demand*.

valuation The estimated value or price of a property.

value-in-use The present worth of a property's future benefits.

■ PASS-POINT CHECKLIST

- ■ **Characteristics of Real Estate**
    - ■ Economic Characteristics
    - ■ Physical Characteristics

- ■ **Real Estate—The Business of Value**
    - ■ Supply and Demand
    - ■ Factors Affecting Supply
    - ■ Factors Affecting Demand

- ■ **Appraisal**
    - ■ Types of Value
    - ■ Market Value
    - ■ Approaches to Appraisal

- ■ **Comparative Market Analysis**

- ■ **The Real Estate Agent's Role**
    - ■ Basic Principles of Value

- ■ **The Three Approaches to Value**
    - ■ The Direct Sales Comparison Approach
    - ■ The Cost Approach
    - ■ The Income Capitalization Approach
    - ■ Reconciliation

- ■ **The Appraisal Process**

- ■ **The Profession of Appraising**
    - ■ Licensing and Certification

■ PRACTICE QUESTIONS

1. All of the following are economic characteristics of land, *EXCEPT*
   a. improvements.
   b. scarcity.
   c. indestructibility.
   d. area preference.

2. The present worth of a property's future benefits defines its
   a. price.
   b. market value.
   c. demand.
   d. value.

3. The price commanded by a property in an arm's-length transaction between informed parties is its
   a. present value.
   b. market value.
   c. demand.
   d. depreciation.

4. The effect of a run-down, low-valued property on neighboring home values is referred to as
   a. progression.
   b. deterioration.
   c. plottage.
   d. regression.

5. An estimate of value based on the expenditure required to replace the subject property is used in which of the methods of appraisal?
   a. Cost approach
   b. Market data approach
   c. Income capitalization approach
   d. Direct sales comparison approach

6. The method of appraisal that would focus on the amount of rent generated by the subject property is the
   a. cost approach.
   b. market data approach.
   c. income capitalization approach.
   d. direct sales comparison approach.

7. A loss of value over time due to physical, functional or locational factors is referred to as
   a. income capitalization.
   b. depreciation.
   c. market price.
   d. situs.

8. A six-bedroom home with a single bathroom would most likely suffer from
   a. external obsolescence.
   b. economic obsolescence.
   c. physical deterioration.
   d. functional obsolescence.

9. The exterior brick walls of a seaside property have been seriously damaged by exposure to the salty air. The resulting depreciation in the property's value is due to
   a. external obsolescence.
   b. economic obsolescence.
   c. physical deterioration.
   d. functional obsolescence.

10. A study of recent comparable sales designed to assist a seller in establishing a listing price is a characteristic of a(n)
    a. income capitalization approach to value.
    b. direct sales comparison approach to value.
    c. comparative market analysis.
    d. subject property valuation study.

15

HUMAN RIGHTS AND FAIR HOUSING

■ **TOPIC REVIEW**

Which federal laws regulate equal housing opportunity?

■ Civil Rights Act of 1866
■ Title VIII of the Civil Rights Act of 1968 (Federal Fair Housing Act)

What is the difference between the Civil Rights Act of 1866 and the Federal Fair Housing Act?

■ The *Civil Rights Act* prohibits all racial discrimination.
■ The *Fair Housing Act* bars discrimination in the sale or rental of residential property on the basis of:

   ■ race
   ■ sex
   ■ color
   ■ national origin
   ■ religion
   ■ handicap
   ■ familial status

What is a discriminatory action?

■ Examples of discriminatory actions include the following, if involving one of the protected classes:

   ■ Refusal to deal with an individual or group
   ■ Changing the terms of a real estate or loan agreement
   ■ Offering different services
   ■ Statements or advertising that indicates a discriminatory restriction
   ■ Any action that indicates an attempt to limit a property's availability

No exceptions apply to real estate brokers.

No exceptions apply to racial discrimination.

What are New York's laws governing fair housing?

- The *New York Executive Law* offers expanded protection against discrimination on the basis of age and marital status, and includes commercial real estate transactions.
- Blockbusting is specifically prohibited by *New York Department of State* regulations.
- *The New York Real Property Law* prohibits discrimination based on the presence of children, and forbids the eviction of a tenant because of pregnancy or a new child. The prohibitions apply to mobile homes.
- New York law specifically exempts public housing aimed at a specific age group; rental of rooms to a single sex; rental of rooms in owner-occupied housing; rental restrictions to persons 55 and over. Licensees may not take *any* part in exempt transactions, and *no exemptions apply to race*.
- Local laws may expand fair housing protections further: New York City, Albany, Syracuse, and Westchester include sexual orientation as a protected class.

What is the American with Disabilities Act (ADA)?

- Enacted in 1992 to protect disabled persons from discrimination in public accommodations, commercial facilities, and multifamily housing of four or more units. It also requires easy access in new construction.

How are discrimination complaints handled?

- A complaint that arises under the *Fair Housing Act* is reported to HUD. After investigating the basis of the complaint, HUD may issue a charge, which may be heard in a federal district court or handled administratively within HUD.
- Complaints arising under the *Civil Rights Act of 1866* are heard in federal court.
- A lawsuit arising under *state law* may be initiated privately, a complaint may be filed with the New York Division of Human Rights and a complaint may be filed with the Department of State for alleged discriminatory acts involving a licensee.

What penalties may be imposed for discriminatory actions?

- Administrative relief under the *Fair Housing Act* includes:
  - injunction
  - $10,000 for a first violation
  - $25,000 for a second violation within 5 years
  - $50,000 for additional violations within 7 years
- Federal district court relief under the *Fair Housing Act* includes:
  - injunction
  - actual and punitive monetary damages, with no dollar limit
  - legal fees and court costs
- *Civil Rights Act of 1866* provides for:
  - injunctive relief
  - monetary damages, with no dollar limit

What are the applicable statutes of limitations?

- ■ *Federal Fair Housing Act*: a charge must be filed with HUD within one year of the alleged act; a federal suit must be brought within two years of the act.
- ■ *Civil Rights Act of 1866*: New York's three-year statute of limitations for torts applies.
- ■ Complaints must be filed with the *New York Division of Human Rights* within one year.

Are there other antidiscriminatory guidelines for licensees?

- ■ The National Association of REALTORS® has adopted a Code for Equal Opportunity that suggests standards of conduct for NAR members to follow in ensuring compliance with fair housing laws.

■ KEY TERMS GLOSSARY

affirmative marketing agreement (NAR) Program to inform all buyers in a minority community about housing opportunities available, without discrimination.

Americans with Disabilities Act (ADA) Federal law requiring reasonable accommodations and accessibility to goods and services for persons with disabilities.

blockbusting The illegal practice of inducing homeowners to sell their property by making representations regarding the entry or prospective entry of minority persons into the neighborhood.

cease and desist order Legal prohibition issued to stop a party from engaging in an activity.

Civil Rights Act of 1866 Federal law that prohibits racial discrimination in the sale and rental of property.

Code for Equal Opportunity Professional standard of conduct for fair housing compliance, promulgated by the National Association of REALTORS® (NAR).

Department of Housing and Urban Development (HUD) Federal agency that administers the Fair Housing Act of 1968.

Executive Law New York State Human Rights Law.

Fair Housing Partnership Agreement Voluntary agreement between NAR and HUD to cooperate in identifying fair housing problems, issues, and solutions.

familial status A fair-housing protected class based on the presence of children in a family.

Federal Fair Housing Act of 1968 The federal law that prohibits discrimination in housing based on race, color, religion, sex, handicap, familial status or national origin. Amended in 1989 to include persons with physical and mental disabilities, and those with children under age 18.

marital status Under New York law, sellers or landlords may not base their decisions on whether or not the prospective occupants are married. A legally protected class.

New York Human Rights Law State law prohibiting discrimination in housing.

New York State Division of Human Rights Agency with which a complaint of housing discrimination may be filed within one year of the alleged act.

protected classes Groups of individuals who have been found to be in need of protection by federal, state, or local laws and regulations against discriminatory actions or conditions.

Real Property Law New York law governing the real estate profession, including prohibitions against discrimination in housing.

redlining The illegal practice of a lending institution denying loans or restricting their number for certain areas of a community.

reverse discrimination Housing discrimination, usually based on quotas, designed by a municipality to achieve a racial balance perceived as desirable.

steering The illegal practice of channeling home seekers to particular areas for discriminatory ends.

testers Members of civil rights and neighborhood organizations, often volunteers, who observe real estate offices to assess compliance with fair housing laws.

■ PASS-POINT CHECKLIST

- ■ **Equal Opportunity in Housing**

- ■ **Federal Fair Housing Laws**
    - ■ Federal Fair Housing Act of 1968
    - ■ *Jones v. Mayer*
    - ■ Equal Housing Poster
    - ■ Blockbusting and Steering
    - ■ Redlining
    - ■ Threats or Acts of Violence
    - ■ Americans with Disabilities Act of 1992

- ■ **New York Human Rights Law**
    - ■ Local Regulations

- ■ **Code for Equal Opportunity**
    - ■ Voluntary

- ■ **Implications for Brokers and Salespersons**

■ PRACTICE QUESTIONS

1. All of the following are protected classes under the federal Fair Housing Act, *EXCEPT*
   a. religion.
   b. sexual orientation.
   c. sex.
   d. familial status.

2. Under the Federal Fair Housing Act, which of the following exemptions apply to real estate brokers?
   a. Transactions involving the sale of single-family homes
   b. Rental transactions involving dwellings with fewer than four units
   c. Rental transactions involving dwellings with fewer than six units
   d. Absolutely no exemptions apply to brokers

3. All of the following are permitted exemptions under the federal Fair Housing Act, *EXCEPT*
   a. sale of a single-family home by the owner.
   b. rental of units in an owner-occupied 3-unit dwelling.
   c. discrimination by a religious organization on the basis of membership in the religion.
   d. racial discrimination based on a broker's good-faith intent to preserve the ethnic character of a neighborhood.

4. In 1996, an individual violated the federal Fair Housing Act for the first time and was fined. In 1999, the individual committed another discriminatory action that violated the Act. What is the maximum fine that may be imposed on this individual in 1999?
   a. $10,000
   b. $15,000
   c. $20,000
   d. $25,000

5. In the previous question, what would be the maximum fine if the individual committed another violation in the year 2001?
   a. $10,000
   b. $25,000
   c. $50,000
   d. $75,000

6. If an individual violates the Civil Rights Act of 1866, what is the maximum monetary penalty he or she may have to pay?
   a. $25,000
   b. $50,000
   c. Only injunctive relief is available under the Civil Rights Act of 1866, not monetary damages.
   d. There is no limit to the monetary damages available for a violation of the Civil Rights Act of 1866.

7. Informing buyers in a minority community about all available housing opportunities is a practice known as
   a. blockbusting.
   b. reverse discrimination.
   c. affirmative marketing.
   d. steering.

8. Inducing homeowners to sell their properties by suggesting that minority persons have or are about to move into the neighborhood is a practice known as
   a. blockbusting.
   b. reverse discrimination.
   c. affirmative marketing.
   d. steering.

16

ENVIRONMENTAL ISSUES

What is asbestos?

■ Asbestos is a mineral used in the past as an insulating material, mostly on plumbing pipes and heating/cooling ducts.

■ It poses a health threat only when disturbed, in which case asbestos dust and fibers may be released into the air.

How can an asbestos problem be fixed?

■ Removal: must be performed by professionals under special conditions

■ Encapsulation: sealing the asbestos with paint or plastic

What are the main sources of lead poisoning?

■ Lead-based paint

■ Lead pipes

What must owners of pre-1978 properties do to comply with the lead-paint disclosure law?

■ Disclose the location of any known lead-based paint

■ Provide buyers or tenants with any reports concerning lead-based paint in the property

■ Provide buyers or tenants with a copy of a special informational pamphlet prepared by the federal government

■ Allow buyers or tenants 10 days to have the property tested for lead-based paint

■ Neither owners nor landlords are required to test for or eliminate lead-based paint

What is radon, and how can it be eliminated?

■ Radon is a naturally-occurring radioactive gas; it may be linked to lung cancer.
■ Improved ventilation systems or exhaust fans may eliminate the hazard posed by concentrations of radon in enclosed areas.

What is mold?

■ A form of bacteria that grows in moist environments. Some varieties are toxic, others are harmless. New York City has legislation regulating mold remediation but there are no federal standards or guidelines established yet.

What are the phases of an environmental assessment?

■ Phase I: General investigation to determine whether or not hazardous substances are present (and where they are concentrated)
■ Phase II: Detailed investigation to confirm contamination
■ Phase III: Clean-up or containment
■ Phase IV: Continuing maintenance and management of environmental hazards

What is CERCLA?

■ The federal Comprehensive Environmental Response, Compensation, and Liability Act
■ CERCLA established Superfund to finance the clean up of hazardous waste sites
■ Establishes owner liability for the cost of cleaning up contaminated property

How is liability established under Superfund?

■ When the Environmental Protection Agency (EPA) becomes aware of a contaminated site, it identifies the potentially responsible parties (PRPs). The PRPs may voluntarily cooperate, or the EPA may begin clean-up activities on its own initiative and recover its costs from the PRPs.
■ If the EPA cleans up the site and the PRPs refuse to reimburse the agency, a court may order them to pay triple damages.
■ Superfund liability is (1) strict, (2) joint and several, and (3) retroactive. That means each historic (retroactive) owner of the property is individually liable for the entire cost of clean up, or the owners (or some of them) may agree to share the costs.

What did SARA accomplish?

■ The innocent landowner defense established under the Superfund Amendments and Reauthorization Act (SARA) exempts qualified past or present owners from liability.
■ SARA provided more funding for Super-fund and clarified lender liability issues.

What laws regulate underground storage tanks?

■ The federal Resource Conservation and Recovery Act (tanks over 1,100 gallons)

■ The New York Underground Storage Tank Act (tanks over 1,000 gallons)

■ KEY TERMS GLOSSARY

asbestos Commonly-used insulating mineral that becomes toxic when it is exposed and fibers and dust are released into the air.

asbestosis Lung disease arising from exposure to asbestos.

building-related illness (BRI) Symptoms such as hypersensitivity, asthma and allergic reactions caused by toxic substances and pathogens in a building that remain with the affected individual even when he or she is away from the building (see sick building syndrome).

chlordane An insecticide once in common use, but banned in the 1980s.

chlorofluorocarbons (CFCs) Gases produced by propellants once used in aerosol sprays and the common coolant, freon. CFCs are linked to depletion of the earth's ozone layer.

Clean Air Act Federal environmental law that prohibits the use of freon in refrigerators and spray cans.

Comprehensive Environmental Response, Compensation, and Liability Act (CERCLA) A federal law administered by the Environmental Protection Agency that establishes a process for identifying parties responsible for creating hazardous waste sites, forcing liable parties to clean up toxic sites, bringing legal action against responsible parties, and funding the abatement of toxic sites.

due diligence A fair and responsible measure of care.

electromagnetic field (EMF) Invisible energy fields created by the movement of electrical currents in high tension wires and electrical appliances. EMFs may be prove to be a potential health hazard but no standards of measurement have been established.

environmental impact statement A report that details the effect of a proposed development on the environment.

Environmental Protection Agency (EPA) A federal agency involved with the problems of air and water pollution, noise, pesticides, radiation, and solid-waste management. EPA sets standards, enforces environmental laws, conducts research, allocates funds for sewage-treatment facilities and provides technical, financial, and managerial assistance for municipal, regional, and state pollution control agencies.

freon A chemical substance once in common household use that is prohibited because it contributes to air pollution.

friable Easily crumbled (i.e., asbestos insulation).

groundwater Surface runoff and underground water systems.

hazardous substances Materials such as chemicals, industrial and residential byproducts, biological waste, and other pollutants that pose an actual or suspected threat to human health, quality of life, and the environment.

landfill A site for the burial, layering, and permanent storage of waste material, consisting of alternating layers of waste and topsoil.

lead poisoning Illness, including the impairment of physical and mental development in children and aggravated blood pressure in adults, resulting from the ingestion of lead toxins, primarily in paint or plumbing.

Leaking Underground Storage Tanks (LUST) Federal environmental protection program to protect the nation's groundwater by identifying underground tanks and preventing or correcting leakage of hazardous materials.

percolation test Test of soil's ability to process waste water prior to installing a septic system.

pollution Artificially-created environmental impurity.

polychlorinated biphenyls (PCBs) Potentially hazardous chemical used in electrical equipment, principally transformers.

potentially responsible parties Under Superfund, the landowners suspected of contaminating a property.

radioactive waste Hazardous by-product of uses of radioactive materials in energy production, medicine, and scientific research.

radon gas Odorless, naturally-occurring radioactive gas that becomes hazardous when trapped and accumulated in unventilated areas of buildings. Long-term exposure to radon is suspected of causing lung cancer.

Safe Drinking Water Act Federal law requiring local public water suppliers to periodically test the quality of drinking water.

septic system Wastewater treatment and disposal system used by individual households.

sick building syndrome (SBS) Range of symptoms, such as asthma, coughing, and hoarseness, that are related to the individual's presence in the affected building, but that disappear when he or she is not exposed to the building's environment.

State Environmental Quality Review Act (SEQRA) The New York state Environmental Quality Review Act, which requires environmental impact statements for certain projects.

Superfund Amendments and Reauthorization Act (SARA) An amendatory statute that contains stronger cleanup standards for contaminated sites, increased funding for Superfund, and clarifications of lender liability and innocent landowner immunity.

termites Wood-boring insects whose presence causes structural damage.

underground storage tanks Buried containers used for storage or disposal of chemicals, fuel, and gas that pose an actual or potential environmental hazard in the event of a leak.

urea formaldehyde foam insulation (UFFI) Carcinogenic insulation material, which is no longer used.

■ PASS-POINT CHECKLIST

■ **Pollution and Environmental Risks in Real Estate Transactions**

■ **Long-Standing Issues**
- Water
- Waste Disposal Sites
- Septic Systems
- Termites
- Asbestos
- Lead Poisoning
- Radon Gas
- Indoor Air Quality
- Polychlorinated Biphenyls (PCBs)

■ **Future Concerns**
- Underground Tanks
- Electromagnetic Fields
- Chlorofluorocarbons
- Mold

■ **Environmental Assessments**

■ **Legal Considerations**
- Superfund Amendments and Reauthorization Act (SARA)
- Underground Storage Tanks
- Implications of Environmental Law

■ **Liability of Real Estate Professionals**

■ PRACTICE QUESTIONS

1. Asbestos poses a health hazard only when it
   a. is used in paint, primarily in pre-1978 homes.
   b. builds up in poorly ventilated areas.
   c. is released into the air as dust and fibers.
   d. is released into the groundwater.

2. What is a common source of lead contamination?
   a. Underground storage tanks
   b. Plumbing pipe insulation
   c. Paint, plumbing pipes, and airborne particles
   d. Electromagnetic fields

3. An owner is required by federal law to do all the following, *EXCEPT*
   a. disclose the location of known lead paint.
   b. test for the presence of lead-based hazards.
   c. give a special pamphlet to buyers and tenants.
   d. allow a 10-day inspection period.

4. Contamination of a site is confirmed in which phase of an environmental assessment?
   a. Phase I   c. Phase II
   b. Phase III   d. Phase IV

5. Liability under Superfund is
   a. limited to the current owner of record.
   b. joint and several, but not retroactive.
   c. voluntary, but not strict.
   d. joint and several, strict, and retroactive.

6. Due diligence is the responsibility of
   a. all the professionals involved in the transaction.
   b. the buyer.
   c. the attorney.
   d. the real estate agent.

7. The ability of soil to process waste water is tested by
   a. percolation.   c. septic systems.
   b. PRPs.   d. the EPA.

8. An artificially created environmental impurity is the definition of
   a. radon gas.
   b. hazardous substances.
   c. pollution.
   d. SBS.

9. Impaired physical and mental development in children is a symptom of
   a. exposure to radon.
   b. lead poisoning.
   c. sick building syndrome.
   d. prolonged exposure to EMFs.

10. Which of the following is a potentially hazardous chemical used in electrical transformers?
   a. PCBs   c. Radon
   b. CFCs   d. Lead

17

REAL ESTATE MATHEMATICS

■ TOPIC REVIEW

How do I convert a percentage to a decimal or a fraction?

■ To convert a percentage to a decimal, move the decimal point two places to the left, and drop the % sign.

■ To covert a percentage to a fraction, place the percentage over 100, and find the highest number by which both can be evenly divided.

A percentage problem has three parts: percentage, total, and part. What if I only know two of them?

■ Whole = part/percent
■ Part = percent/whole
■ Percent = part/whole

How do I compute area?

■ To determine a square or rectangular area, use this formula:
$$\text{area} = \text{depth} \times \text{width}$$

How do I compute volume?

■ To determine the cubic capacity of an area, use this formula:
$$\text{volume} = \text{length} \times \text{width} \times \text{height}$$

■ KEY TERMS GLOSSARY

acre A measure of land equal to 43,560 square feet, 4,840 square yards, 4,047 square meters, 160 square rods, or 0.4047 hectares.

front foot The measurement of a parcel of land by the number of street of feet or road frontage.

hectare 10,000 square meters (about 2.471 acres).

■ PASS-POINT CHECKLIST

- ■ **Percentages**
- ■ **Rates**
- ■ **Areas and Volumes**
- ■ **Land Units and Measurements**

■ PRACTICE QUESTIONS

1. What is the total cost of a driveway 15' wide, 40' long and 4" thick if the concrete costs $60.00 per cubic yard and the labor costs $1.25 per square foot?
   - **a.** $527.25
   - **b.** $693.75
   - **c.** $1,194.00
   - **d.** $1,151.75

2. If your monthly rent is $525, what percent would this be of an annual income of $21,000?
   - **a.** 25%
   - **b.** 30%
   - **c.** 33%
   - **d.** 40%

3. Find the number of square feet in a lot with a frontage of 75 feet, 6 inches, and a depth of 140 feet, 9 inches.
   - **a.** 10,626.63
   - **b.** 10,652.04
   - **c.** 216.25
   - **d.** 25,510.81

4. A salesperson sells a property for $58,500. The contract he has with his broker is 40% of the full commission earned. The commission due the broker is 6%. What is the salesperson's share of the commission?
   - **a.** $2,106
   - **b.** $1,404
   - **c.** $3,510
   - **d.** $2,340

5. What is the interest rate on a $10,000 loan with semiannual interest of $450?
   - **a.** 7%
   - **b.** 9%
   - **c.** 11%
   - **d.** 13.5%

6. A warehouse is 80' wide and 120' long with ceilings 14' high. If 1,200 square feet of floor surface has been partitioned off, floor to ceiling, for an office, how many cubic feet of space will be left in the warehouse?
   - **a.** 151,200
   - **b.** 134,400
   - **c.** 133,200
   - **d.** 117,600

7. If the broker received a 6.5% commission that was $5,200, what was the sales price of the house?
   - **a.** $80,400
   - **b.** $80,000
   - **c.** $77,200
   - **d.** $86,600

8. The seller received a $121,600 check at closing after paying a 7% commission, $31,000 in other closing costs and the $135,700 loan payoff. What was the total sales price?
   - **a.** $288,300
   - **b.** $306,300
   - **c.** $308,500
   - **d.** $310,000

9. A fence is being built to enclose a lot 125' by 350'. If there will be one 10' gate, how many running feet of fence will it take?
   - **a.** 465
   - **b.** 600
   - **c.** 940
   - **d.** 960

10. If you purchase a lot that is 125' × 150' for $6,468.75, what price did you pay per front foot?
    - **a.** $23.52
    - **b.** $43.13
    - **c.** $51.75
    - **d.** $64.69

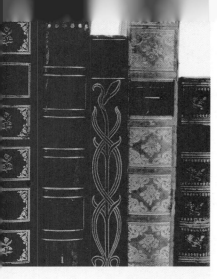

18

INDEPENDENT CONTRACTOR/EMPLOYEE

■ TOPIC REVIEW

What is the difference between an employee and an independent contractor?

■ Employees are subject to day-to-day control over how they perform their jobs. Their salaries are subject to tax withholding (income and Social Security).

■ Employees (not independent contractors) can be covered by employer-paid unemployment insurance and workers comp programs.

■ Brokers are not required to withhold taxes from payments made to independent contractors, and independent contractors are subject to a lesser degree of employer control: employers may dictate the outcome, but not the means used to achieve it.

What makes a licensee an employee or an independent contractor?

■ The distinction depends on the conduct of the parties. Under both federal and New York law, a written agreement is strong evidence of the intent to create an independent contractor relationship.

■ The manner of compensation is a factor. Employees are paid for hours worked; independent contractors are compensated for performance.

■ The degree of control a broker may exercise over an employee is greater than the control that may be exercised over an independent contractor.

■ If the individual participates in employer-funded health care benefits, pension plans, sick leave, or paid vacation time, he or she is likely to be considered an employee.

What is an employer?

■ The employer is always the sponsoring broker. The agent and broker mutually decide on the status to become either an employee or an independent contractor, but not both.

What are antitrust laws, and how do they affect the real estate brokerage business?

- Antitrust laws such as the Sherman Antitrust Act of 1890 prohibit any unreasonable restraint of trade due to cooperation or conspiracy of members of the trade.

What are the types of activities prohibited by antitrust laws?

- Price-fixing
- Group boycotting
- Market allocation

How do federal antitrust laws apply to the real estate profession?

- Brokers who work for separate, competing brokerages may not discuss commission rates, set a standard industry rate, or publish commission rates.
- Brokers may not join together to engage in group boycotts of other brokers.

■ KEY TERMS GLOSSARY

employee A person who works as a direct employee of an employer, and who has employee status for income tax, insurance, and benefits purposes. The employer is obligated to withhold income taxes and social security taxes from an employee's compensation.

group boycott An agreement among members of a trade to exclude other members from fair participation in the activities of the trade.

independent contractor A person who is retained to perform a certain act, but who is subject to the control and direction of another only with regard to the end result and not as to the way in which the act is performed. Unlike an employee, an independent contractor pays for all expenses, and Social Security and income taxes, and receives no employee benefits.

market allocation An agreement among members of a trade to refrain from competition in specific market areas.

price-fixing An agreement between members of a trade to artificially maintain prices at a set level.

restraint of trade The unreasonable restriction of business activities as the result of the cooperation or conspiracy of members of the trade.

■ PASS-POINT CHECKLIST

- **Salesperson Employment Status**
  - Employee Status
  - Independent Contractor Status
  - Tests of Employment
- **Antitrust Laws**

■ PRACTICE QUESTIONS

1. Two brokers who work for the same firm meet and decide to charge the same set commission rate to all of their sellers. Is their action illegal?
   a. Yes, because it constitutes a violation of the antitrust laws.
   b. Yes, because a broker's commission must be related to the costs involved in any single transaction.
   c. No, because the brokers do not represent competing firms.
   d. No, because antitrust laws do not apply to commission rates of MLS membership fees.

2. The classification of a licensee as an employee or an independent contractor depends on all of the following factors, *EXCEPT*
   a. the licensee's conduct.
   b. the broker's conduct.
   c. the terms of a written agreement.
   d. the number of hours worked.

3. A broker typically would provide which of the following for an independent contractor?
   a. Workers compensation
   b. Health insurance
   c. Errors and omissions insurance
   d. Office space

4. All of the following are included in the IRS safe-harbor guidelines that define independent contractors in the real estate industry, *EXCEPT*
   a. income based on sales output.
   b. written contract.
   c. licensed as a broker or salesperson.
   d. access to unemployment insurance and workers compensation benefits.

5. Which of the following is a characteristic of an independent contractor?
   a. Employer pays income and social security tax
   b. Compensation based on dollars-per-hour
   c. Extensive employer control
   d. Compensation linked to performance

6. All of the following contract provisions are required for independent contractor status for real estate licensees under New York law, *EXCEPT*
   a. the licensee will not receive compensation based on hours worked.
   b. the licensee may work out of his or her home.
   c. the licensee may terminate the agreement at any time.
   d. the licensee must work during specific set hours.

7. The employment contract between a broker and a salesperson should be renewed
   a. monthly.
   b. quarterly.
   c. annually.
   d. every two years.

8. Over coffee, several competing brokers agree that a set commission rate, applied to everyone, would result in better service for consumers. The brokers agree to use the same rate in order to improve the quality of real estate in their town. Have these brokers committed an antitrust violation?
   a. Yes, they have engaged in illegal price-fixing.
   b. No, their agreement does not constitute a restraint of trade.
   c. Yes, they have entered into a group boycott of nonparticipating firms.
   d. No, this in a traditional and legal way of doing business.

9. Two competing brokerages agree to limit their business activities to different areas of town, with their two "territories" clearly drawn on the map. Which antitrust violation does this represent?
   a. Group boycotting
   b. Market allocation
   c. Redlining
   d. Price-fixing

10. An independent contractor must
    a. comply with the broker's policy.
    b. attend office meetings.
    c. take office duty when assigned.
    d. meet a specific sales quota.

19

THE BROKER'S OFFICE

■ TOPIC REVIEW

Who needs to have a real estate license?

■ When an individual lists, sells, purchases, negotiates, exchanges, leases, rents, or auctions real estate, or negotiates the sale of a business involving substantial real estate for another person and for a fee, he or she must hold a real estate broker's license.

■ A New York attorney, or individuals who perform real estate related services for one person only, are not required to have a real estate license. Neither are public officers when performing their duties, persons who are acting under court order, or business brokers.

What are the qualifications for a real estate broker's license?

■ Salespersons who have completed an apprenticeship under a managing broker and taken a 45-hour brokerage business to be conducted.

■ The Department of State issues several classes of license, depending on the type, form, and scope of brokerage business to be conducted.

What are the broker's responsibilities?

■ The sponsoring broker is responsible for the training, supervision, and management of all real estate activities of the salesperson and or associate broker.

■ The sponsoring broker may not profit by the misdeeds of his agent.

■ The broker owes his client absolute fidelity, care, and in accordance with the clients needs and wishes (see CC-LOAD Chapters 2 and 3).

When are licenses renewed?

■ All broker and salesperson licenses are for a two-year period.

■ Successful completion of 22-1/2 hours of continuing education is required during the two-year license period.

What are antitrust laws and how do they affect the real estate brokerage business?

- Antitrust laws prohibit any unreasonable restraint of trade due to cooperation or conspiracy of members of the trade.
- Antitrust laws include the Sherman Antitrust Act of 1890 and the Clayton Antitrust Act.

What are the types of activities prohibited by antitrust laws?

- Price-fixing
- Group boycotting
- Market allocation
- Tie-in arrangements

How do federal antitrust laws apply to the real estate profession?

- Brokers who work for separate, competing brokerages may not discuss commission rates, set a standard industry rate, or publish commission rates.
- Brokers may not join together to engage in group boycotts of other brokers.
- Multiple listing services may not deny any interested party reasonable access to their service. While MLSs may have membership requirements and fees, the requirements must be reasonable, and any membership fee must be related to the costs incurred by the service. No MLS may engage in discriminatory practices.
- An MLS may not restrict its members' business activities (by requiring that they not join any other MLS, for example, or not cooperate with non-member brokers). MLSs may not regulate the business hours of its members or limit the kinds of properties members may advertise.

How may a brokerage office be formally organized?

- Sole proprietorship: broker is the only owner, and is entitled to all the earnings (and liable for all the debts and losses).
- Corporation: an "artificial person" created by state law. Shareholders own the business but are not liable for its debts. A corporation continues to exist when its shareholders die, but its income is "double taxed" at both the corporate and shareholder level.
- S corporation: A special form of corporation that avoids double taxation. There are strict rules on the number of shareholders and the sources of income permitted.
- General partnership: A business in which two or more owners undertake a business for profit, sharing equally in the operation, profits, and losses.
- Limited partnership: A form of partnership in which a general partner is responsible for operating the business, and limited partners play a more passive investor role.
- Limited liability company (LLC): A form of state-sanctioned business organization that combines the limited liability of a corporation with a partnership's tax advantages.

May a brokerage firm ever act as a dual agent?

■ Yes. The New York Department of State permits a brokerage firm to function as a dual agent if both the buyer and the seller are fully informed of the dual agency and give their consent. An agent of the firm may be appointed the designated agent of each party. The firm is a dual agent, but the designated agents function as single agents of their respective clients. Designated agency agreements should be made in writing to avoid confusion.

■ KEY TERMS GLOSSARY

antitrust laws Laws designed to prevent the unreasonable restraint of trade as a result of the cooperation or conspiracy of various members of the trade or business.

Article 12A of the Real Property Law Regulations relating to real estate licensees.

blind ad An advertisement that does not indicate that it was placed by a licensee.

consent decree An agreement by which one party promises not to commit an illegal act in the future while not admitting that it was committed in the past.

designation An award recognizing special training and expertise, given by professional organizations.

employee A person who works as a direct employee of an employer, and who has employee status for income tax, insurance and benefits purposes. The employer is obligated to withhold income taxes and social security taxes from an employee's compensation.

fair employment laws Laws designed to prevent employers from making their hiring and firing decisions on factors unrelated to job performance.

group boycott An agreement among members of a trade to exclude other members from fair participation in the activities of the trade.

independent contractor A person who is retained to perform a certain act, but who is subject to the control and direction of another only with regard to the end result and not as to the way in which the act is performed. Unlike an employee, an independent contractor pays for all expenses, Social Security and income taxes, and receives no employee benefits.

market allocation An agreement among members of a trade to refrain from competition in specific market areas.

multiple listing service A marketing organization composed of member brokers who agree to share their listings with one another in the hope of procuring ready, willing and able buyers more quickly and efficiently.

policy and procedures guide A written statement of a company's history, goals, rules, and guidelines for conducting the firm's business.

price-fixing An agreement between members of a trade to artificially maintain prices at a set level.

restraint of trade The unreasonable restriction of business activities as the result of the cooperation or conspiracy of members of the trade.

Sherman and Clayton Antitrust Acts Federal legislation that prohibits anti-competitive business practices.

tie-in arrangement An arrangement by which provision of certain products or services is made contingent on the purchase of other, unrelated products or services.

vicarious liability Liability that is created not because of a person's actions but because of the relationship between the liable person and other parties.

■ PASS-POINT CHECKLIST

- ■ **Who Needs a License**
- ■ **Other Related Licenses**
- ■ **Who Does Not Need a License**
- ■ **Obtaining a License**
  - ■ The Broker's Application
  - ■ Experience Requirement
- ■ **Renewal of License**
- ■ **Review of Chapter 1**
  - ■ Advertising Guidelines
- ■ **Antitrust Laws**
  - ■ Commissions
  - ■ Group Boycotts
  - ■ Market Allocation
  - ■ Tie-in Agreements
  - ■ Enforcement
  - ■ Risk Reduction
- ■ **Multiple-Listing Services**
  - ■ Access to MLS
- ■ **Independent Contractor Status**
  - ■ Exemption from Business Taxation
- ■ **The Broker's Responsibility to Manage and Supervise**
  - ■ Organization of the Brokerage Company
  - ■ Recruiting Licensees
  - ■ Training
  - ■ Policy and Procedures Guide
  - ■ The Supervision Requirement
- ■ **Audits for Compliance**
- ■ **Professional Organizations**
  - ■ New York State Association of REALTORS®
- ■ **Law of Agency**

■ PRACTICE QUESTIONS

1. Two brokers who work for the same firm meet and decide to charge the same set commission rate to all their sellers. Is their action illegal?
   a. Yes, because it constitutes a violation of the antitrust laws.
   b. Yes, because a broker's commission must be related to the costs involved in any single transaction.
   c. No, because the brokers do not represent competing firms.
   d. No, because antitrust laws do not apply to commission rates or MLS membership fees.

2. The classification of a licensee as an employee or an independent contractor depends on all the following factors, *EXCEPT*
   a. the licensee's conduct.
   b. the broker's conduct.
   c. the terms of a written agreement.
   d. the number of hours worked.

3. In which of the following activities may an MLS legally engage?
   a. Restricting the type of properties that may be advertised
   b. Regulating the business hours of members
   c. Charging a fee for membership
   d. Prohibiting membership in other MLS organizations

4. An arrangement by which provision of certain products or services is made contingent on the purchase of other, unrelated products or services is referred to as
   a. a tie-in.
   b. designation.
   c. market allocation.
   d. a group boycott.

5. Which of the following is a characteristic of an independent contractor?
   a. Employer pays income and social security tax
   b. Compensation based on dollars-per-hour
   c. Extensive employer control
   d. Compensation linked to performance

6. A brokerage's history, goals, rules, and guidelines for conducting its business are usually stated in a(n)
   a. policy and procedures guide.
   b. MLS.
   c. independent contractor agreement.
   d. standard written employment agreement.

7. Employers are prevented from making their hiring and firing decisions based on factors unrelated to the employee's job performance by
   a. antitrust laws.
   b. policy and procedures guide.
   c. fair employment laws.
   d. vicarious liability.

8. The GRI designation is awarded to qualified individuals by
   a. the New York Department of State.
   b. an accredited college or university.
   c. the New York Office of Accreditation and Designation.
   d. the New York State Association of REALTORS®.

9. The unreasonable restriction of business activities as the result of the cooperation or conspiracy of members of the trade is known as
   a. market allocation.
   b. restraint of trade.
   c. multiple listing.
   d. group boycotting.

10. Vicarious liability is created by
    a. the relationship between the liable person and others.
    b. participation in an MLS.
    c. antitrust laws.
    d. a written agreement between an independent contractor and his or her employer.

20

REAL ESTATE FINANCE II

■ TOPIC REVIEW

How is a mortgage used in New York?

■ New York is a lien theory state. In New York, a mortgage simply represents the pledging of the property as security of a loan. The mortgagee (lender) does not hold actual title. In case of default, formal and lengthy legal process is required for the mortgagee to obtain title to the pledged property.

■ In title theory states, a mortgagee is given actual title to the property by the mortgagor (borrower). The document is referred to as a trust deed, rather than a mortgage. In case of default, it is simple for the mortgagee to take possession of the property, because it already holds legal title to it.

What are the types of mortgages?

■ A purchase-money mortgage refers to any loan used for the original purchase of property.

■ Shared-equity mortgages are loans in which a lender's interest is secured by the promise of receiving a share of any profits realized when the property is sold.

■ Package loans include both real and personal property.

■ Open-end mortgages permit the borrower to take out additional loans.

■ blanket mortgages include more than one property.

■ A wraparound mortgage is a new loan that includes, but does not replace, an existing loan.

■ A subordinate mortgage, such as a home equity loan, is a junior mortgage recorded after an original loan.

What are the types of commercial financing?

■ Bullet loans are loans with a term of 3 to 5 years.

■ Miniperm loans offer variable rates and interest accrual that permit borrowers to enjoy greater cash flow during the early years.

■ Floating rate loans with accrual are similar to residential adjustable-rate mortgages.

■ Participation loans are similar to residential share-equity loans: they permit the lender to earn revenue from a project's income and sale.

■ Land-leasebacks provide developers with the equity necessary to construct an improvement on their land. The developer sells the land to an investor, who leases it back for development.

■ Joint ventures create a partnership between the investor and the borrower. Normally, the investor provides the financing and the borrower does the development work.

What are construction loans?

■ Construction loans are used to finance the construction of improvement on property.

■ The loan is short-term (usually 6 months to 3 years) and temporary—when the construction is completed, the construction loan is replaced with some form of permanent financing.

■ Construction funds are normally disbursed to the borrower in a series of increments, called draws, over the course of the project. Alternatively, the lender may pay bills as they are submitted by the borrower. The borrower is charged interest on the loan funds only after they are disbursed.

■ Once the project is built, a takeout loan is used to pay off the construction lender.

What is a sale-leaseback?

■ A sale-leaseback is a form of commercial financing in which a property is sold to an investor and then immediately leased back to the original owner.

When does the economy influence the real estate industry?

■ When interest and unemployment rates rise, real estate market activity (sales and financing) decline. When interest rates and unemployment fall, the real estate market enjoys increased activity.

■ The economic factors that influence the real estate cycle include:
  ■ Supply and demand
  ■ Population characteristics and demographic trends
  ■ Social attitudes
  ■ Property value fluctuations

■ The real estate cycle is also affected by government activity, such as regulation and taxation. Decisions of the Federal Reserve System regarding interest rates directly impact the real estate market.

■ KEY TERMS GLOSSARY

blanket mortgage A mortgage covering more than one parcel of real estate, providing for each parcel's partial release from the mortgage lien upon repayment of a definite portion of the debt.

bridge loan A short-term loan designed to cover a gap between the sale of one property and the purchase of another (also called a swing loan, temporary loan, or interim financing).

bullet loan A short- or intermediate-term (3 to 5 years) interest-only loan with a balloon payment at the end of the term (also called an intermediate loan or conduit financing).

construction loan A short-term loan made during the construction phase of a building project (also referred to as interim financing).

disintermediation A tight-money real estate lending market (in which real estate loans are more difficult to obtain) that results when investors choose to invest in stocks, bonds, and mutual funds rather than savings accounts, limiting the funds available to lenders.

FHA loan Loan insured by the Federal Housing Administration and made by an approved lender under FHA's regulations.

Freddie Mac (FHLMC) Federal Home Loan Mortgage Corporation: a corporation established to purchase primarily conventional mortgage loans in the secondary mortgage market.

Fannie Mae (FNMA) Federal National Mortgage Association: a quasi-government agency established to purchase any kind of mortgage loans in the secondary mortgage market from the primary lenders.

Ginnie Mae (GNMA) Government National Mortgage Association: a government agency that plays an important role in the secondary mortgage market; sells mortgage-backed securities backed by pools of FHA and VA loans.

home equity loan A loan (sometimes called a line of credit) under which a property owner uses his or her residence as collateral and can then draw funds up to a prearranged amount against the property.

imputed interest An IRS concept that treats some concessionary low-interest loans as if they had been paid and collected at a statutory rate.

index With an adjustable-rate mortgage, a measure of current interest rates; a basis for calculating the new rate at the time of adjustment.

joint venture The joining of two or more people to conduct a specific business enterprise.

negative amortization Gradual building up of a large mortgage debt when payments are not sufficient to cover interest due and reduce the principal.

open-end mortgage A mortgage loan that is expandable to a maximum dollar amount, the loan being secured by the original mortgage.

package loan A real estate loan used to finance the purchase of both real property and personal property, such as in the purchase of a new home that includes carpeting, window coverings, and major appliances.

participation loan A mortgage in which the lender participates in the income of the mortgaged venture.

private mortgage insurance (PMI) Insurance that limits a lender's potential loss in a mortgage default, issued by a private company rather than by the FHA.

purchase-money mortgage A note secured by a mortgage or deed of trust given by a buyer, as borrower, to a seller, as lender, as part of the purchase price of the real estate.

sale and leaseback agreement A transaction in which an owner sells his or her improved property and, as part of the same transaction, signs a long-term lease to remain in possession of the premises.

secondary mortgage market A market for the purchase and sale of existing mortgages, designed to provide greater liquidity of mortgages.

shared-equity mortgage Loan in which the purchaser receives assistance (such as help with the down payment, a reduced interest rate, or help with monthly payments) from a partner (such as a lender, relative, or the seller), who receives a share of the profit when the property is eventually sold.

swing loan A short term loan similar to a bridge loan that uses the strength of the borrower's equity in the property he or she is selling, to purchase a new property.

takeout loan A loan commitment obtained prior to a lender extending a construction loan, under the terms of which the takeout lender will pay off the construction loan once the work is finished. Provides assurance for the construction lender that the initial short term loan will be satisfied.

underwriting The process by which a lender evaluates a prospective borrower's application through verification of employment and financial information and analysis of credit and appraisal reports.

VA mortgage A mortgage loan on approved property made to a qualified veteran by an authorized lender and guaranteed by the Department of Veterans Affairs to limit the lender's possible loss.

wraparound mortgage An additional mortgage in which another lender refinances a borrower by lending an amount including the existing first mortgage amount without disturbing the existence of the first mortgage.

■ PASS-POINT CHECKLIST

- **The Use of the Mortgage**
- **Home Mortgages**
- **Types of Mortgages**
- **Broker's Issues in Real Estate Finance**
    - Commercial Financing
    - Construction Loans
    - Sale-Leasebacks
- **Ground Leases**
- **FHA Financing**
- **The Economy and Real Estate Cycles**
    - Economic Influences
- **Recent Developments**
    - Condominiums and Cooperatives
    - Loan Processing

■ PRACTICE QUESTIONS

1. New York is a "lien theory state." That means
   a. if the borrower defaults, the lender can quickly obtain possession without lengthy legal proceedings.
   b. the lender (or a third party) holds the mortgage in trust until the mortgage is paid off.
   c. the mortgage is a pledge of the property as security for a loan, rather than a transfer of title.
   d. the mortgagee may not foreclose on the property.

2. The most common type of loan used for the original purchase of property is
   a. blanket mortgage.
   b. purchase-money mortgage.
   c. home equity loan.
   d. shared-equity mortgage.

3. All of the following forms of loans involve a lender taking an interest in the profits realized by a property's operation or sale *EXCEPT*
   a. shared-equity mortgage.
   b. participation loan.
   c. joint venture.
   d. home equity loan.

4. What type of mortgage includes more than one property?
   a. Package loan
   b. Blanket mortgage
   c. Wraparound mortgage
   d. Shared-equity mortgage

5. What type of loan includes both real and personal property?
   a. Package loans
   b. Blanket mortgages
   c. Shared-equity loans
   d. Bridge loans

6. Which of the following statements is true regarding construction loans?
   a. Construction loans are usually long-term.
   b. Construction loans are usually paid to the borrower in one lump sum.
   c. Construction loans are short-term and temporary.
   d. When construction is complete, the construction loan continues as before.

7. All of the following statements are true regarding payments to a borrower in a construction loan, *EXCEPT*
   a. payments are provided in a lump sum.
   b. payments are often released in a series of draws.
   c. payments are often made when bills are submitted.
   d. interest on the loan applies only when draws are paid out.

8. A form of commercial financing in which a property is sold to an investor and then immediately leased by the original owner is a
   a. participation loan.
   b. buyback arrangement.
   c. sale-leaseback.
   d. joint venture.

9. When interest and unemployment rates rise, real estate market activity
   a. increases.
   b. decreases.
   c. is unaffected.
   d. may either increase or decrease.

10. The Federal Reserve System makes decisions regarding what factor that affects the real estate market?
    a. Demographics
    b. Interest rates
    c. Unemployment rates
    d. Supply and demand

CHAPTER TWENTY-ONE

21

REAL ESTATE INVESTMENTS

■ TOPIC REVIEW

What makes real estate an attractive option for investors?

- Real estate offers a high rate of return
- Investments in real estate provide a hedge against inflation
- Leveraging and pyramiding
- Tax advantages

Are there any disadvantages to real estate investment?

- Low liquidity (money is tied up in the investment)
- High risk
- Expertise required
- Active investor involvement in maintaining and operating the property

How is the return on a real estate investment calculated?

- Gross Rental Income
  - operating expenses
  = *Net Operating Income*
- Net Operating Income
  - debt service
  = *Cash Flow*
- Cash Flow
  + mortgage amortization
  + appreciation
  + tax benefits
  = *Total Return on Investment*

What is the difference between an operating statement and a pro forma?

- An operating statement is a record of a property's actual past performance as a generator of income.
- A pro forma is a projection or estimate of a property's likely performance in the future.

Are leveraging and pyramiding the same thing?

- To leverage an investment, the investor makes as small a down payment as possible, and takes out a mortgage loan with low interest rates, payable over a long term. The investor's expectation is that the property will increase in value or generate sufficient income to allow the investor to make a profit while still repaying the loan. Essentially, leveraging is using as little of the investor's own money as possible to generate the greatest possible return on the investment.
- Pyramiding involves an investor refinancing properties already owned, and using the proceeds to purchase additional properties. The investor is able to increase his or her investment holdings with a minimal use of his or her own money.

How do individuals invest in real estate?

- Investment syndicates
- General partnerships
- Limited partnerships
- Real estate investment trusts (REITs)
- Real estate mortgage investment conduits (REMICs)

How are real estate investments evaluated?

- Holding period
- Resale potential
- Discounted cash-flow analysis
- Net present value
- Internal rate of return

How is depreciation used as a tax reduction tool?

- Depreciation permits investors to recover an asset's basis over its useful life.
- Only improvement costs may be recovered; not the land cost itself.
- While shelter advantages are limited, tax credits are permitted for low-income housing projects.

What is the difference between capital gain and adjusted basis?

- Capital gain is the investor's taxable profit when the investment is sold.
- Adjusted basis is the original cost of the property, plus the cost of any improvements, minus any claimed depreciation.

How does a property exchange work to the advantage of the real estate investor?

■ As long as the property received by the investor in the exchange has a value equal to or greater than the original property, the investor is permitted to defer the taxable realized gain until the property is sold.

■ Cash or property received in the exchange is referred to as boot, and is subject to tax.

How else may an investor defer federal income tax on the gain realized in the sale of a real estate investment?

■ By conveying the investment property in an installment sale, the investor may defer tax on gain realized from the sale as a whole.

■ KEY TERMS GLOSSARY

adjusted basis Basis minus depreciation.

appreciation An increase in the worth or value of a property due to economic or related causes, which may prove to be either temporary or permanent.

basis The cost that the Internal Revenue Service attributes to an owner of an investment property for the purpose of determining annual depreciation and gain or loss on the sale of the asset.

boot Money or property given to make up any difference in value or equity between two properties in an exchange.

capital gain Profits realized from the sale of assets such as real estate.

cash flow The net spendable income from an investment.

cost recovery An Internal Revenue Service term for depreciation.

current rent roll A list of present tenants and their rents.

debt service Mortgage payments, including principal and interest on an amortized loan.

depreciation In appraisal, a loss of value in property due to any cause including physical deterioration, functional obsolescence, and locational obsolescence.

discounted cash flow analysis Mathematical model of variables inherent in an investment.

discounting Method for mathematically calculating present value of money, based on time and the discount rate.

discount rate Rate of return needed to compensate an investor for risk; the Federal Reserve's loan rate for eligible banks.

disposition Investment strategy for reconciling anticipated gain or loss with the risk involved.

general partnership A typical form of joint venture in which each general partner shares in the administration, profits, and losses of the operations.

gross operating income In income property, rent that is actually collected.

gross rental income Total income from rents, before expenses.

holding period The time an investment or asset is possessed.

installment sale a transaction in which the sales price is paid two or more installments over two or more years. If the sale meets certain requirements, a taxpayer can postpone reporting such income until future years by paying tax each year only on the proceeds received that year.

internal rate of return (IRR) Discount rate that, when applied to both positive and negative cash flows, results in zero net present value.

leverage The use of borrowed money to finance the bulk of an investment.

limited liability company (LLC) Business entity that permits members to enjoy the tax benefits of a partnership combined with the limited liability of corporations.

limited liability partnership (LLP) Partnership form that permits investors to enjoy the tax benefits of a partnership combined with the limited liability of corporations.

limited partnership Partnership administered by one or more general partners and funded by limited or silent partners who are by law responsible for losses only to the extent of their investments.

marginal tax rate The percentage rate at which the last dollar of income is taxed.

mortgage debt service A property owner's mortgage payment.

negative cash flow Negative figure resulting when expenditures on an investment exceed the income it produces.

net operating income (NOI) The income projected for an income-producing property after deducting losses for vacancy and collection and operating expenses.

net present value (NPV) Difference between the present value of all positive and negative cash flows.

passive income Income derived from an investment activity in which the investor does not take an active management or participatory role.

pro forma statement Statement of hypothetical future operating revenues and expenses; a projection of income and loss.

pyramid Investment strategy of refinancing existing properties and using the borrowed money.

rate of return The ratio between earnings and cost.

real estate investment syndicate Business organization in which individuals combine their resources to invest in, manage, or develop a particular property.

real estate investment trust (REIT) Trust ownership of real estate by a group of individuals who purchase certificates of ownership in the trust.

real estate mortgage investment conduit (REMIC) A tax vehicle created by the Tax Reform Act of 1986 that permits certain entities that deal in pools of mortgages to pass income through to investors.

return The income from a real estate investment, calculated as a percentage of cash invested.

Section 1031 property exchange A tax-deferred exchange of like-kind investment or commercial property.

silent partner A partner who does not assist in managing an enterprise, and whose losses are limited to his or her initial investment.

straight-line depreciation A method of calculating depreciation for tax purposes, computed by dividing the adjusted basis of the property by the estimated number of years of remaining useful life.

tax basis The original cost basis for property, less depreciation and plus the amount spent on capital improvements.

tax credit A direct reduction in tax payable, as opposed to a deduction from income.

tax depreciation Straight-line depreciation: cost decided by years.

tax shelter A property whose income-tax losses can offset other income to minimize taxes.

■ PASS-POINT CHECKLIST

- **The Nature of Real Estate Investment**
- **Preparing to Be an Investor**
    - Leverage
    - Risk and Reward
- **Analyzing Property Income**
    - Operating Statements
    - Current Rent Roll
    - Pro Forma Statements
- **Investment Ownership Structure**
    - Forms of Syndicates
    - Real Estate Investment Trusts
    - Real Estate Mortgage Investment Conduits
- **Holding Period and Disposition**
- **Types of Investment Properties**
- **Investment Analysis Techniques**
    - Discounted Cash-Flow Analysis
- **Income Tax Considerations**
    - Depreciation
    - Capital Gains
    - Exchanges
    - Tax Credits
    - Installment Sales

■ PRACTICE QUESTIONS

1. All the following are attractive characteristics of real estate investment, *EXCEPT*
   a. low liquidity.
   b. high return.
   c. leveraging potential.
   d. inflation hedge.

2. Which of the following formulas correctly expresses cash flow?
   a. Gross rental income – operating expenses
   b. Appreciation + mortgage amortization
   c. Gross rental income – operating expenses – debt service
   d. Net operating income – mortgage amortization + appreciation

3. An investor who wanted to forecast future performance of a property would most likely rely on which of the following resources?
   a. Operating statement
   b. Pro forma
   c. Gross rental income statement
   d. Leveraging

4. The original cost of a property, plus the cost of any improvements, minus claimed depreciation, represents which of the following?
   a. Basis
   b. Capital gain
   c. Depreciation
   d. Adjusted basis

5. The cost that the IRS attributes to an owner of an investment property for the purpose of determining annual appreciation and gain or loss on the asset's sale is the property's
   a. basis.   c. depreciation.
   b. capital gain.   d. adjusted basis.

6. In an exchange of like-kind property, one investor exchanged a building for a similar building plus $100,000 in cash. The cash is referred to as
   a. basis.   c. leverage.
   b. boot.   d. passive income.

7. The net spendable income generated by an investment property is referred to as its
   a. capital gain.
   b. cash flow.
   c. net present value.
   d. adjusted basis.

8. A form of joint venture in which each participant shares in the administration, profits, and losses of the operation of an investment property is a
   a. limited partnership.
   b. REMIC.
   c. real estate investment trust.
   d. general partnership.

9. A business entity that combines the tax benefits of a partnership with the limited liability of a corporation is a(n)
   a. IRR.   c. LLC.
   b. REIT.   d. REMIC.

10. Which of the following investment entities was created by the Tax Reform Act of 1986?
    a. REMIC   c. IRR
    b. REIT   d. LLP

22

GENERAL BUSINESS LAW

What are the principal sources of law in the United States?

■ The principal sources of law in the U.S. are the Constitution, federal laws, state constitutions, state laws, local ordinances, federal regulations, state regulations, and state and federal court decisions.

What is "commercial paper"?

■ Commercial paper, also called negotiable instruments, refers to written promises or orders for the payment of money. Commercial paper is negotiable, which means it can be transferred from one person to another by one of four types of endorsement: blank, restrictive, special, and qualified. The UCC defines commercial paper as including notes, drafts, checks, and certificates of deposit.

What are the requirements for commercial paper?

■ In writing
■ Signed by the maker or drawer
■ Payable to the bearer or a specific payee
■ For a specific sum of money at a specific time or on demand

What is a partnership?

■ A partnership is an association of two or more people as common owners to carry on a for-profit business. Liability is unlimited, and profits and losses are passed directly through to the owners.

What is a corporation?

■ A corporation is the formation of a new, legal person owned by shareholders, formed when the secretary of state approves a certificate of incorporation.

Liability is limited, the business is managed by a board of directors elected by shareholders, and profits are taxed twice: once at the corporate level and once when the shareholders receive dividends.

How can double-taxation be avoided?

■ Organization as an S Corporation, limited liability company, or limited liability partnership provides owners with the limited liability protection of the corporate form without the tax burden of dual taxation.

How are courts organized?

■ The federal court system is divided into district courts, specialized courts, courts of review, and the Supreme Court. There are four federal district courts in New York, and appeals in federal cases are heard by the second circuit court of appeals.

■ In New York, the state supreme court is the lowest of general jurisdiction. The highest in the state is the court of appeals. Small claims court is a court of local jurisdiction.

What is the difference between civil and criminal law?

■ Criminal law governs injuries against society or the state. Civil law is concerned with injuries committed by individuals against each other's person or property.

■ Arbitration and mediation are faster and more efficient means to resolve disputes between individuals.

■ KEY TERMS GLOSSARY

administrative law Laws regulating the way in which government agencies conduct their activities.

administrator A person appointed by a court to oversee the estate of a person who died intestate.

arbitration A hearing in which a person selected or appointed hears and resolves a dispute.

bankruptcy A federal court procedure in which a debtor is relieved of certain liabilities.

case law Law established by court decisions.

civil law Laws regarding wrongs committed by one person against another.

commercial law An area of law concerning business and industry.

commercial paper Written notes, checks, and certificates of deposit, such as promises to pay money.

common law The body of law based on custom, usage, and court decisions.

constitutional law Law that arises from federal and state constitutions.

contract law Laws concerning contracts between parties.

corporation law Laws dealing with how a corporation is created, operated, and dissolved.

criminal law Law that defines crimes and provides for punishment.

due process Legal procedures designed to protect the rights of individuals.

endorsement The act of signing the back of a check or note.

executor A person, corporate entity, or other type of organization designated in a will to carry out its provisions.

financing statement See Uniform Commercial Code.

injunction A court-order issued to restrain one party from doing a specific act.

litigation Legal action in a court of law.

mediation A method for resolving disputes in which the mediator guides the parties into agreement.

negotiable instrument A written promise or order to pay a specific sum of money that may be transferred by endorsement or delivery. The transferee then has the original payee's right to payment.

personal property law Law governing chattels.

Real Property Law The New York law that governs the real estate profession.

security agreement A document in which personal property is pledged as security of repayment of a debt.

small claims court A local court in which disputes are settled without attorneys or high court costs.

statute of limitations That law pertaining to the period of time within which certain actions must be brought to court.

statutory law Law established by legislatures.

torts A civil wrong committed by one person against another.

trustee The holder of bare legal title in a deed of trust loan transaction.

trusts and wills A fiduciary arrangement whereby property is conveyed to a person or institution, called a trustee, to be held and administered on behalf of another person, called a beneficiary. The one who conveys the trust is called the trustor.

Uniform Commercial Code A codification of commercial law, adopted in most states, that attempts to make uniform all laws relating to commercial transactions, including chattel mortgages and bulk transfers. Security interests in chattels are created by an instrument known as a security agreement. To give notice of the security interest, a financing statement must be recorded. Article 6 of the code regulates bulk transfers—the sale of a business as a whole, including all fixtures, chattels, and merchandise.

■ PASS-POINT CHECKLIST

- ■ **Sources of Law**
- ■ **Uniform Commercial Code**
- ■ **Negotiable Instruments**
- ■ **Business Organizations**
  - ■ Partnerships
  - ■ Corporations
  - ■ Security Offerings
- ■ **The Federal Court System**
- ■ **New York Court System**
- ■ **Substantive and Procedural Law**
- ■ **Civil Law**
  - ■ Civil Procedure
  - ■ Dispute Resolution
  - ■ Bankruptcy
  - ■ Estates
  - ■ Divorce in New York
- ■ **Statute of Limitations**

■ PRACTICE QUESTIONS

1. Which of the following sources of law is created by local governing bodies?
   a. Constitutions
   b. Regulations
   c. Decisions
   d. Ordinances

2. What does the statement, "Commercial paper is negotiable," mean?
   a. Must be made in writing
   b. It may be transferred from one person to another
   c. It cannot be endorsed
   d. Its value is uncertain

3. All of the following are requirements for commercial paper, *EXCEPT*
   a. it must be made in writing.
   b. it must be signed by the maker or drawer.
   c. it must be approved by the secretary of state.
   d. it must be made for a specific sum of money.

4. Shareholder ownership, dual taxation and management by a board of directors are all characteristics of a(n)
   a. partnership.
   b. corporation.
   c. limited liability company.
   d. S corporation.

5. An association of two or more people as common owners to carry on a business for profit is the definition of a(n)
   a. corporation.
   b. limited liability company.
   c. partnership.
   d. S corporation.

6. Owners may enjoy limited liability and avoid dual taxation by organizing as a(n)
   a. corporation.
   b. limited liability company.
   c. partnership.
   d. S corporation.

7. The federal court system is divided into how many types of courts?
   a. two   c. four
   b. three   d. six

8. How many federal district courts are there in New York?
   a. two   c. four
   b. three   d. six

9. In New York, what court is the highest court in the state?
   a. Supreme court
   b. District court
   c. Small claims court
   d. Court of appeals

10. Which type of law governs injuries against society or the state?
    a. Civil
    b. Criminal
    c. Small claims
    d. Ordinances

CONSTRUCTION AND DEVELOPMENT

■ TOPIC REVIEW

What are the different roles of planners, developers, and sub-dividers?

■ Planners establish the framework for communities or developments, including amenities, transportation, infrastructure, population density, and growth goals.

■ Subdividers buy undeveloped land, then divide it into individual parcels for development.

■ The subdivider prepares a plat of subdivision, illustrating the property by lots and blocks and detailing streets and utility easements.

■ Restrictions may be imposed on how the lots may be used to maintain the subdivision's planned character.

■ The completed plat must be approved by local officials, and recorded in the county in which the land is located.

■ Developers build improvements (such as homes or commercial buildings) on subdivided lots.

■ Many developers also market the new properties, while others rely on local real estate professionals.

Are there any limits on land development?

■ Developments must comply with local master plans.

■ Land-use plans are subject to approval by local planning boards or commissions.

■ Developments in environmentally-sensitive areas may require environmental impact studies and detailed environmental audits.

How can a subdivider maximize open space and control density?

■ Varying street patterns: the use of gridiron, loop, radius, or curvilinear street patterns creates different environments and changes the density of housing development.

■ Cluster planning: by clustering private lots around central cul-de-sacs, open public space can be enhanced with little or no loss of housing density.

What laws regulate subdivided land?

■ Interstate Land Sales Full Disclosure Act: This federal law requires certain developers (those who are engaged in interstate transactions or who lease 25 or more units) to register their projects with HUD.

■ The law further requires that developers provide prospective purchasers with specific, detailed information at least three business days prior to the signing of any sales contract.

■ In New York, for installment sales of subdivided land, the developer must file with the Department of State, and an informational offering statement must be furnished to prospective buyers.

■ When a subdivision includes at least five lots, a water and sewerage plan must be approved by the Department of Health. Developments of 500 or more lots must include a municipal water system.

What are the characteristics of a condominium?

■ Condominiums are a form of fee simple ownership. The condominium owner holds a fee simple interest in his or her own unit, plus an undivided interest in the common elements (stairways, parking garages, etc.). Condominium owners are free to take out mortgages, and they receive individual tax bills.

■ Condominium owners do not bear any direct financial liability for any adjoining units.

■ The common elements are managed and administered by an association, funded by monthly fees.

■ Condominiums are governed by written regulations called by-laws.

What is a cooperative?

■ In a cooperative, a corporation owns the building. Each unit owner holds a personal property interest in the building in the form of shares of the corporation, and a proprietary lease to his or her individual apartment.

■ Individual owners equitably share responsibility for the corporation's debts and liabilities.

■ The corporation may reject applicants for any reason except the Fair Housing classes.

■ Owners of a cooperative are called the shareholders.

How is a condominium or cooperative established?

■ A condominium or cooperative may be built new, or an existing building or community may be converted.

■ In New York, a developer or sponsor who plans to construct or convert to a cooperative or condominium project must first file the plan with the county clerks office and wait for the attorney general's office review.

- In New York City and portions of Westchester, Nassau, and Rockland counties, a minimum of 15 percent of existing tenants must purchase their units or the conversion may not occur.
- In New York, more than half of the tenants must demonstrate the intent to purchase their units if the developer plans to evict existing tenants when their leases expire.
- Persons with disabilities and persons over age 62 may not be evicted in a condominium or cooperative conversion.

What is a town house development?

- A town house development includes elements of both cooperative and condominium ownership: owners hold their units and the underlying land in fee simple. All common elements (including open land) are owned by a homeowners association, made up of unit owners.

What is time-sharing?

- Time-sharing is the purchase of a fractional ownership interest in a resort or vacation property for a specified portion of the year.
- Time-sharing is regulated by New York's blue-sky securities statute.
- Purchasers are entitled to a 10-day right of rescission.

■ KEY TERMS GLOSSARY

board of directors Elected managing body of a corporation, specifically of a cooperative apartment building.

board of managers Elected managing body of a condominium.

bylaws Rules and regulations adopted by an association.

common elements Parts of a property normally in common use by all of the condominium residents.

completion bond A bond furnished to ante completion of a project.

conversions Process by which an existing residential property is changed into a cooperative or condominium.

covenants, conditions, and restrictions (CC&Rs) Provisions in condominium by-laws restricting the owner's usage of the property.

curvilinear system Street pattern system that integrates major arteries with smaller winding streets and cul-de-sacs.

declaration A formal statement of intention to establish a condominium.

density zoning Local ordinances that limit the number of housing units that may be built per acre within a subdivision.

Department of Environmental Conservation (DEC) Agency that issues permits for developments in or around a protected wetland or other environmentally-sensitive area.

developer One who improves land with buildings, usually on a large scale, and sells to homeowners and/or investors.

disclosure statement Document that must be filed by the developer of a new or converted condominium or cooperative project, including an architect's or engineer's evaluation of the structure, an expense statement, prices per unit, and other financial and administrative information.

environmental impact study Report detailing the effect of a proposed development on the existing environment, including possible alternative measures to remedy or repair environmental damage.

eviction plan Method of converting a rental property into a condominium or cooperative, in which existing tenants will be evicted when their leases expire.

gridiron pattern Street pattern systems that evolved out of the government rectangular survey, featuring a regular grid of straight-line streets and alleys.

impact fees Charges levied by a local government to help the community absorb the public costs involved in the development of a new subdivision.

Interstate Land Sales Full Disclosure Act Federal law that regulates the sale of certain real estate in interstate commerce.

noneviction plan Method of converting a rental property into a condominium or cooperative.

planned unit development (PUD) A planned combination of diverse land uses such as housing, recreation, and shopping in one contained development or subdivision.

planning board Municipal body overseeing orderly development of real estate.

plat of subdivision A map of a subdivision indicating the location and boundaries of individual properties, streets, and easements.

preliminary prospectus Description of new or converted condominium or cooperative property, subject to change, available for inspection by present tenants after review by the attorney general (also referred to as a red herring).

proprietary lease A written lease in a cooperative apartment building, held by the tenant (shareholder), giving the right to occupy a particular unit.

public offering A transaction falling under the jurisdiction of the New York attorney general's office, requiring certain specific transactional and financial disclosures. The sale of any form of shared housing in New York is a public offering.

reserves Funds set aside by, for instance, a condominium board, to cover possible large expenses.

sponsor The developer of a new or converted condominium or cooperative.

subdivider One who buys undeveloped land, divides it into smaller, usable lots and sells the lots to potential users.

subdivision A tract of land divided by the owner, known as the *subdivider*, into blocks, building lots and streets according to a recorded subdivision plat.

time-sharing Undivided ownership of real estate for only a portion of the year.

wetland survey An intensive examination of property, coordinated by the U.S. Army Corps of Engineers, to determine whether or not it should be classified and protected as a wetland.

■ PASS-POINT CHECKLIST

- ■ **Construction Standards**
  - ■ Federal Agencies
  - ■ State Agencies
  - ■ Regional Agencies

- ■ **The Role of the Real Estate Agent**

- ■ **Building Inspections**

- ■ **Subdivision**
  - ■ Restrictions on Land Use
  - ■ Environmental Regulations
  - ■ Value of Land for Subdivision

- ■ **The Process of Subdivision**

- ■ **Costs and Financing**

- ■ **Restrictive Covenants**
  - ■ Enforcement of Deed Restrictions
  - ■ Types of Subdivisions and Subdivision Density

- ■ **Land-Use Regulations**
  - ■ Building Codes
  - ■ Interstate Land Sales Full Disclosure Act
  - ■ New York State Subdivided Land Sales Law

- ■ **Condominiums**
  - ■ Selling Condominiums

- ■ **Cooperative Ownership**

- ■ **Condominium/Cooperative Construction and Conversion**
  - ■ Conversion Restrictions

- ■ **Town Houses, PUDs and Time-Sharing**

■ PRACTICE QUESTIONS

1. A person who buys a single parcel of land and then separates it into multiple lots, is a
   a. planner.
   b. developer.
   c. subdivider.
   d. sponsor.

2. Which of the following street patterns is based on a land survey system developed by the federal government?
   a. Radius
   b. Gridiron
   c. Curvilinear
   d. Public space

3. The Interstate Land Sales Full Disclosure Act applies to interstate transactions or developers who lease how many units?
    a. 10 or fewer
    b. 15 or more
    c. 25 or more
    d. 50 or more

4. In New York, a developer of subdivided land sold on an installment basis must file certain information with which agency?
    a. HUD
    b. Dept. of State
    c. DEC
    d. Dept. of Real Estate

5. A form of ownership in which an individual has a fee simple interest in certain real property, plus an undivided co-ownership of common areas is a
    a. condominium.
    b. cooperative.
    c. time-share.
    d. conversion.

6. If a New York City developer wants to convert an existing rental building into a condominium by evicting tenants as their leases expire, what is the minimum percentage of current tenants who must express their intent to purchase their units
    a. 15
    b. 33
    c. 51
    d. 75

7. All of the following statements are true of time-shares in New York, *EXCEPT*
    a. time-sharing is regulated by the securities statute.
    b. purchasers are entitled to a 30-day right of rescission.
    c. time-sharing is undivided ownership of a property for only a portion of the year.
    d. the blue-sky law governs time-shares.

8. The process by which an existing residential property becomes a cooperative or condominium is
    a. declaration.
    b. eviction.
    c. subdivision.
    d. conversion.

9. An intensive examination of property to determine whether it should be classified as a wetland is referred to as a(n)
    a. wetland plat.
    b. prospectus.
    c. wetland survey.
    d. environmental audit.

10. An individual who holds a proprietary lease most likely occupies a unit in a
    a. cooperative.
    b. condominium.
    c. time-share resort.
    d. PUD.

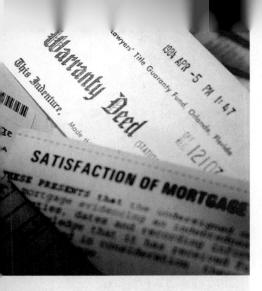

24

CONVEYANCE OF REAL PROPERTY

■ TOPIC REVIEW

What is title?

■ Title to real estate means the right to ownership of the land. It also refers to evidence of that ownership.

How may title to real estate be transferred?

■ Voluntary alienation: transferred by gift or sale during the owner's life
■ Involuntary alienation: transferred without the owner's consent by act of the state (such as condemnation or escheat), a court (foreclosure or judgment sale), or an individual (adverse possession)
■ By will: testamentary succession to the testator's devisees through probate
■ Descent: transferred by law to the statutory heirs of an owner who dies without a will (intestate)

How may land be transferred by act of nature?

■ Accretion is the increase in a property due to the movement of land by the natural forces of wind and water.
■ Erosion is the slow decrease in a property due to the natural forces of wind and water.
■ Avulsion is the sudden decrease in property due to natural forces such as earthquakes.

What is adverse possession?

■ A person who has used someone else's land in a manner that is continuous, open, notorious, hostile, and exclusive for ten years without the owner's protest may claim title by adverse possession.
■ Anyone claiming title by adverse possession may perfect their claim by bringing a suit to quiet title.

■ Successive, continuous users may combine their periods of adverse possession to meet the statutory 10-year requirement through the process of tacking.

What is testamentary succession?

■ When a deceased owner of real estate has made a valid will, he or she is said to have died testate.

■ Because title to property transferred by testamentary succession passes automatically to the devisees, named in the will, the heirs or devisees do not usually receive a deed.

■ Although title passes automatically to the persons named in the will, they cannot take possession until after the estate has been through probate.

What is probate?

■ Probate is a surrogate court proceeding to rule on the validity of a will, the identity of the devisees and the portions of the estate due to each.

What happens to real property if its owner dies without making a will?

■ When an owner of real property dies without having made a will (intestate), title to the property passes according to the law of descent and distribution in the state in which the property is located.

■ In New York, an intestate's estate is first applied to the payment of all outstanding debts. The remainder of the estate is distributed to the decedent's spouse, children, grandchildren, parents or siblings, in a descending order depending on the decedent's survivors.

■ While children may be disinherited, a spouse is entitled by New York law to the greater of one-third of the estate, or to $50,000 plus one-half of the remainder of the estate.

■ In New York, if a decedent dies intestate and without heirs, the property escheats to the state.

What are the legal requirements in New York for making a will?

■ Sound mind
■ At least 18 years old
■ Written
■ Signed by the testator in the presence of at least two witnesses

■ KEY TERMS GLOSSARY

adverse possession The actual, visible, hostile, notorious, exclusive, and continuous possession of another's land under a claim of title. Possession for ten years may be a means of acquiring title.

condemnation A judicial or administrative proceeding to exercise the power of eminent domain through which a government agency takes private property for public use and compensates the owner.

dedication The voluntary transfer of private property by its owner to the public for some public use such as for streets or schools.

descent Acquisition of an estate by inheritance in which an heir succeeds to the property by operation of law.

devise A gift of real property by will; the act of leaving real property by will.

escheat The reversion of property to the state or county, as provided by state law, in cases where a person dies intestate without heirs capable of inheriting or when the property is abandoned.

executor A male person, corporate entity, or any other type of organization designated in a will to carry out its provisions.

heir One who might inherit or succeed to an interest in land under the state law of descent when the owner dies without leaving a will.

intestate The condition of a property owner who dies without leaving a valid will.

involuntary alienation Transfer of real estate without the owner's initiative, as in foreclosure or condemnation.

last will and testament An instrument executed by an owner to convey the owner's property to specific persons after the owner's death.

probate Legal proceeding to establish the will of a deceased person.

testate Having made and left a valid will.

testator The (male) maker of a valid will.

testatrix The (female) maker of a valid will.

voluntary alienation Transfer of title by gift or sale according to the owner's wishes.

■ PASS-POINT CHECKLIST

- ■ **Title**
- ■ **Voluntary Alienation**
- ■ **Involuntary Alienation**
  - ■ Condemnation
  - ■ Foreclosure
  - ■ Natural Processes
  - ■ Partition
  - ■ Adverse Possession
- ■ **Transfer of a Deceased Person's Property**
  - ■ Probate Proceedings
  - ■ Transfer of Title by Will
  - ■ Transfer of Title by Descent
- ■ **Title Closing and Costs**

■ PRACTICE QUESTIONS

1. Title to real estate is
   a. only transferred by gift or sale during the owner's lifetime.
   b. the right to and evidence of ownership of the land.
   c. evidence of a claim to property by adverse possession.
   d. passed to persons named in a decedent's will only after probate proceedings are complete.

2. The sudden decrease in a property due to natural forces is referred to as
   a. accretion.
   b. erosion.
   c. avulsion.
   d. succession.

3. What is the correct word used to describe the persons who receive property under a valid will?
   a. Heirs
   b. Testators
   c. Devisees
   d. Descendants

4. Foreclosure and adverse possession are examples of which of the following?
   a. Voluntary alienation
   b. Involuntary alienation
   c. Testamentary succession
   d. Involuntary dedication

5. How many years must a person use another's property to claim title by adverse possession in New York?
   a. 7
   b. 10
   c. 15
   d. 24

6. In New York, if a decedent dies intestate without heirs, what happens to his or her real property?
   a. It passes according to the law of descent and distribution
   b. It escheats to the county in which the real property is situated
   c. It is taken by the state through the legal process known as accretion
   d. It escheats to the state

7. All of the following are legal requirements for an enforceable will in New York, EXCEPT
   a. testator of sound mind.
   b. testator at least 18 years old.
   c. testator may not have a criminal record.
   d. signed in the presence of two witnesses.

8. When listing property for a real estate, the broker must
   a. be certain the client is the actual executor.
   b. report the results of the transaction to the Probate Court.
   c. contact all the heirs for approval.
   d. assume property management duties until the transaction is complete.

9. A male person who is designated to carry out the provisions of a will is referred to as the
   a. testator.
   b. devisor.
   c. executor.
   d. testatrix.

10. A transfer of title by gift or sale according to the owner's wishes is a(n)
    a. partition.
    b. voluntary alienation.
    c. involuntary alienation.
    d. probate.

25

PROPERTY MANAGEMENT

■ TOPIC REVIEW

What is a property manager?

■ A property manager is the general agent of an owner and acts as the administrator of the subject property.

■ Property managers are employed under the terms of a management agreement, which specifically defines the manager's duties and responsibilities and expressly authorizes the manager to act on behalf of the owner.

How does a property manager set rental rates?

■ First, the manager makes a budget, based on estimated operating expenses (which may be either variable or fixed), as well as planned expenditures for renovating or modernizing the property.

■ Then, the manager analyzes both the building's condition and the rental rates charged by comparable properties in the area.

■ Based on these factors (the budgeted expenses and market analysis), the manager can set a rental rate for the property that will cover expenditures and generate an adequate return for the owner.

What are the manager's other responsibilities?

■ Soliciting suitable tenants
■ Collecting rent
■ Maintaining and administering the property
■ Obtaining insurance coverage
■ Hiring, supervising, and firing employees as necessary
■ Keeping financial records and paying taxes on the property
■ Resolving tenant issues

What does building maintenance include?

- Building maintenance includes ensuring the property's physical integrity and seeing that routine upkeep, cleaning, and minor repairs are performed in a timely manner.
- Maintenance also includes more elaborate work, such as adapting interior space to particular tenant needs, ensuring the structural integrity of the property, and conducting renovations and modernizing improvements as necessary.

What are the basic types of insurance coverage for commercial properties?

- Fire and hazard insurance (property and fixtures)
- Business interruption insurance (loss of income)
- Casualty insurance (theft and vandalism)
- Public liability insurance (injuries on the premises)
- Worker's compensation (injured employees)

With which laws should a property manager be especially concerned?

- Local ordinances, such as the Multiple Dwelling Law in New York City and Buffalo, require certain minimum standards of health and safety in multi-unit residential buildings. Other localities have additional regulations.
- New York state regulates mobile home parks.

What are rent control and rent stabilization laws?

- Rent control systems are in effect in all or parts of various municipalities all across New York State.
- Rent control applies to property containing three or more units constructed prior to February 1947.
- In New York City, a maximum base rent for each apartment is adjusted every two years; landlords are permitted to increase rent by 7.5 percent annually until the base rent figure is reached.
- The Division of Housing and Community Renewal regulates rent controls outside New York City, establishing a separate maximum base rent.
- Landlords are permitted to raise controlled rent only if services are increased, major capital improvements are installed, or in the event of hardship or high labor and fuel costs. Rents can be reduced if a landlord fails to maintain the property.
- Outside New York City, rent stabilization is a function of the local adoption of the Emergency Tenant Protection Act (ETPA).
- Stabilization applies to buildings with more than six residential units constructed between February 1947 and January 1, 1971.
- Under rent stabilization, rent increases are established by a local board.

How are property managers designated?

■ The most widely recognized designation is Certified Property Manger (CPM), a professional designation awarded by the Institute of Real Estate Management (IREM).

■ KEY TERMS GLOSSARY

anchor stores Large stores whose presence attracts other tenants to a retail development.

boiler and machinery coverage Insurance policy covering repair and replacement of major equipment and systems such as central air-conditioners and heating plants.

business interruption insurance Insurance policy coverage against a financial loss resulting from a property's inability to generate income.

capital expense Money spent on permanent, value-adding property improvements.

capital reserve budget Money set aside to pay for expected improvements and other expenditures.

casualty insurance Insurance policy coverage against theft, burglary, vandalism, physical damage to systems, and health and accident coverage on a specific-risk basis.

Certified Property Manager (CPM) A real property manager who has completed specific educational requirements, demonstration reports and qualified for the CPM designation, granted by the Institute of Real Estate Management of the National Associaton of REALTORS ®.

contents and personal property insurance Coverage of personal property and other building contents when they are not on the insured premises.

corrective maintenance Repairs made after damage has occurred.

Division of Housing and Community Renewal (DHCR) New York agency that administers rent control and stabilization.

fire and hazard insurance Policy providing coverage for direct loss of or damage to property resulting from fire, storms, hail, smoke, or riot.

industrial property Land and facilities used for manufacturing.

liability insurance Policy covering risks assumed by owners with regard to public entry onto the insured property, including medical expenses due to landlord negligence and injuries sustained by employees in the course of their work (worker's compensation claims).

management agreement Employment contract between property owner and manager, under which the manager assumes the responsibility for administering and maintaining the property as the owner's general agent.

management proposal A property manager's plan for supervising the property, provided to the owner.

market analysis Study undertaken by a property manager of the local and regional market, as well as the underlying property itself, to provide information about the economic conditions, supply, demand, and similar competing properties.

maximum base rent (MBR) Under rent control, the maximum rent allowable for an individual unit.

multiperil policies Insurance policies offering protection from a range of potential perils, such as fire, hazard, public liability, and casualty, in a single policy.

neighborhood analysis Part of a property manager's market analysis focusing on the economy, services, demographics, and transportations amenities of a specific geographical location.

office property Any type of structure (low-rise, highrise, complex, or campus) used by such non-manufacturing, non-retail tenants as medical, legal, and financial professionals.

operating budget A property manager's plan for expenses.

preventative maintenance Maintenance performed to avoid future damage.

property analysis Thorough study of a property's positive and negative attributes, from structural components and systems to services and amenities, and the terms of each individual lease.

property maintenance Array of activities designed to protect a property's structural integrity, long-term physical condition, as well as cleaning, minor carpentry and repairs, scheduled upkeep, and tenant improvement alterations.

property management report A property manager's regular, periodic report to the owner about the property.

property manager Someone who manages real estate for another person for compensation.

regional analysis Study of the economic and demographic character of the larger regional or metropolitan area in which a property is located.

rent control State or local regulations restricting the amount of rent that may be charged for particular properties.

rent stabilization Local regulations that stem from the adoption of the Emergency Tenant Protection Act, and which limit maximum allowable rent increases.

replacement cost The construction cost at current prices of a property that is not necessarily an exact duplicate of the subject property but serves the same purpose or function as the original.

resident manager A property manager who lives on the site managed.

residential property Any type of property used as a dwelling.

retail property Any type of property used for commercial retail purposes, including storefronts, shopping centers, and enclosed malls.

Section 8 Federal housing assistance program administered by the FHA, in which low- and moderate-income tenants pay a fixed portion of their income in rent, with HUD paying the remainder.

security deposit A payment by a tenant, held by the landlord during the lease term and kept (wholly or partially) on default or destruction of the premises by the tenant.

surety bond Bond covering an owner against financial losses resulting from the criminal acts or negligence of an employee in the course of performing his or her job.

workers' compensation acts State laws that require building owners to obtain workers' compensation insurance coverage from a private insurer to protect against claims for damages arising from on-the-job injuries.

■ PASS-POINT CHECKLIST

- ■ **The Property Manager**
- ■ **Types of Property that are Managed**
  - ■ Residential Property
  - ■ Office Space
  - ■ Retail Property
  - ■ Industrial Property
- ■ **The Management Agreement**
- ■ **Functions of the Property Manager**
- ■ **Planning and Budgeting**
  - ■ Market Analysis
  - ■ Budgeting
- ■ **Marketing**
  - ■ Marketing Activities
- ■ **Managing Leases and Tenant Relations**
  - ■ Renting the Property
  - ■ Negotiating Leases
  - ■ Collecting Rents
  - ■ TenantsRights
- ■ **Maintaining the Property**
  - ■ Hiring Employees versus Contracting for Services
- ■ **Owner Relations, Reports, and Insurance**
  - ■ Owner Relations
  - ■ Insurance Coverage
- ■ **Skills Required of a Property Manager**
- ■ **The Management Field**
  - ■ Rent Regulations
  - ■ Rent Control
  - ■ Rent Stabilization

■ PRACTICE QUESTIONS

1. Usually, a property manager represents an owner as what type of agent?
    a. Special   c. Universal
    b. General   d. Limited

2. If an investment property burned down, the owner's lost income would be recovered if the building was covered by which type of insurance?
    a. Casualty
    b. Fire and hazard
    c. Business interruption
    d. Ownerscompensation

3. Rent control regulations apply to
    a. One-unit to three-unit residential properties built before 1945.
    b. Residential properties containing three or more units, constructed before January 1971.
    c. Residential properties containing three or more units, constructed before February 1947.
    d. Residential properties containing six or more units, constructed prior to January 1, 1947.

4. Losses due to theft and vandalism are covered by which type of insurance policy?
    a. Casualty
    b. Fire and hazard
    c. Business interruption
    d. Ownerscompensation

5. Rent stabilization programs apply to
    a. One-unit to three-unit residential properties built between 1945 and 1990.
    b. residential properties containing six or more units, constructed prior to Jan. 1971.
    c. residential properties of six or more units, constructed between Feb. 1947 and Jan. 1, 1971.
    d. residential properties of six or more units, built between Jan. 1, 1945 and Feb. 1, 1970.

6. If a member of the public slipped and fell on the floor of a building's lobby, his or her medical expenses would be covered if the owner had which type of insurance?
    a. Casualty   c. Liability
    b. Contents   d. Surety

7. The employment contract between a property manager and the owner is called a(n)
    a. maintenance agreement.
    b. management agreement.
    c. MBR.
    d. CPM.

8. The part of a property manager's market analysis that focuses on a specific, limited location is what type of analysis?
    a. Regional   c. Property
    b. Neighborhood   d. Block

9. Local rent regulations that stem from the adoption of the Emergency Tenant Protection Act are referred to as
    a. rent control.
    b. maximum base rent regulations.
    c. rent protection.
    d. rent stabilization.

10. A form of insurance that covers an owner against financial losses resulting from the criminal acts or negligence of an employee is
    a. worker's compensation.
    b. surety.
    c. casualty.
    d. liability.

26

TAXES AND ASSESSMENTS

■ **TOPIC REVIEW**

What are the types of real estate taxes?

■ General real estate tax (ad valorem tax): levied by taxing districts (such as schools, water, parks, and sanitary districts), municipalities, counties, and the state. The tax amount is based on the value of each individual property.

■ Special assessments: levied by local assessors on limited areas affected by a public improvement (such as sidewalks or streetlights) to distribute financial responsibility for the improvement among only the home owners who benefit from it.

How is property assessed for tax purposes?

■ Upstate New York assesses property at a uniform percentage of value.

■ New York City and Long Island divide property into four separate taxing categories.

■ Owners may protest assessments they feel are erroneous, or based on incorrect evaluations of their property.

■ An equalization factor is used to achieve uniformity among taxing districts that use different rates; where full-value assessment is used, equalization is not required

■ After assessment, the funds required by the taxing body's budget is divided by the total number of properties on the assessment roll. The result is the tax rate. Each property's tax bill is determined by multiplying assessed valuation by the tax rate.

■ When are tax bills sent out, and how are they paid?

■ Tax bills are sent out at different times, depending on how the taxing body calculates its tax year:

  ■ Town, county, and state taxes: January to December (paid in advance)

  ■ Village taxes: tax year may begin in March or June

- School taxes: levied July 1 to June 30, but payable in arrears or installments
- City taxes: payable in two to four installments

Is any property exempt from taxation?

- Public property (parks, schools, playgrounds, and government buildings)
- Property owned by hospitals and religious or educational institutions (if used for tax-exempt purposes)
- Property owned by persons over age 65 who are on limited incomes is subject to special reductions (10 to 50 percent), determined by local governments.
- Property owned by qualified military veterans may also be eligible for a reduction.
- Special reductions may also be available to encourage industrial, commercial, or residential development, or to preserve agricultural land.

What happens if a property owner fails to pay his or her real estate taxes?

- Penalties, in the form of additional interest charges, are applied to overdue tax bills.
- Unpaid taxes constitute a lien against the offending property.
- Real estate tax liens generally have priority over other liens.
- Unpaid tax liens may be recovered by a tax foreclosure or a tax sale.

What is the difference between a tax foreclosure and a tax sale?

- Tax foreclosure: a proceeding by the taxing body against the property itself (in rem), rather than against the owner.
- In a tax foreclosure, the lienholder takes title to the property, and the former owner loses all rights and interests.
- Tax sale: a public sale conducted by the tax collector. The purchaser of a property sold at a tax sale must pay, at a minimum, the outstanding taxes and penalties.

What is the difference between an equitable and a statutory right of redemption?

- Equitable right of redemption: the delinquent owner is entitled to redeem the property before the tax sale by paying off the lien plus penalties, interest, and other charges.
- Statutory right of redemption: the delinquent owner may also redeem the property for some period (determined by individual municipalities and counties) after the sale.

■ KEY TERMS GLOSSARY

ad valorem tax A tax levied according to value. Also called the general tax.

aged exemption A partial exemption from the school tax, available in New York for low-income elderly homeowners.

appropriation The process of levying property taxes, or setting aside of land in a subdivision.

assessment review board A local body for hearing property-tax protests and empowered to lower or raise assessments.

assessment roll Public record listing assessed value for all real property in a village, town, city, or county.

assessments The imposition of a tax, charge, or levy, usually according to established rates.

equalization factor Factor used to raise or lower assessed values for tax purposes in a county or taxing district to make them equal to assessments in other counties or districts.

full-value assessment Practice of assessing property at its full value, rather than by a percentage of full value.

grievance A complaint.

homestead Land that is owned and occupied as the family home. In many states a portion of the area or value of this land is protected of exempted from judgment for debts.

in rem A proceeding against the realty directly as distinguished from a proceeding against a person.

levy To assess; to seize or collect. To levy a tax is to assess a property and set the rate of taxation. To levy an execution is to officially seize the property of a person in order to satisfy an obligation.

mill One-tenth of one cent. A tax rate of 52 mills would be $.052 tax for each dollar of assessed valuation of a property.

non-homestead Property that is not used as the owner's primary residence buildings with more than four dwelling units, or other nonresidential properties.

statutory redemption period The right of a defaulted property owner to recover the property after its sale by paying the appropriate fees and charges. Varies by area: New York City allows a statutory redemption period of four months.

taxable status date The date on which annual tax assessment rolls are fixed.

tax certiorari An appeal to state court of a local assessment board of review's ruling.

tax foreclosure Legal proceeding (comparable to a private mortgage foreclosure) brought by a taxing body against the property itself (in rem); former owner loses all rights and claims.

tax lien A charge against property created by operation of law. Tax liens and assessments take priority over all other liens.

tax sale A court-ordered sale of real property to raise money to cover delinquent taxes.

true tax Actual taxes payable for a property after all exemptions and reductions for which the property or its owner is qualified.

■ PASS-POINT CHECKLIST

■ Tax Liens
- ■ General Tax (Ad Valorem Tax)
- ■ Special Assessments (Improvement Taxes)
- ■ Exemptions

■ The Taxation Process
- ■ Assessment
- ■ Appropriation
- ■ Enforcement of Tax Liens

■ PRACTICE QUESTIONS

1. A real estate tax levied on a specific area to fund a public improvement is a
   a. general real estate tax.
   b. special real estate tax.
   c. special assessment.
   d. municipal assessment.

2. All of the following property is exempt from property taxes in whole or in part, *EXCEPT*
   a. a public elementary school.
   b. a federal office building.
   c. a nonprofit hospital.
   d. property owned by persons over age 62.

3. A court proceeding against specific real property, but not the property's owner, to recover a real estate tax lien is a
   a. tax sale.
   b. tax foreclosure.
   c. tax lien.
   d. special assessment.

4. A defaulting owner's right to recover his or her real property by paying off the outstanding lien plus penalties and other charges for a certain period after a tax sale, is referred to as a(n)
   a. equitable right of redemption.
   b. statutory right of redemption.
   c. redemption from foreclosure.
   d. equitable right of recovery.

5. The phrase "ad valorem" means
   a. "according to value."
   b. "the thing itself."
   c. "by frontage foot."
   d. "by a percentage of value."

6. One mill is equal to
   a. 1/100th of a dollar.
   b. 1/100th of a cent.
   c. 1/10th of a cent.
   d. 1 percent of one cent.

7. A defaulting owner's right to recover his or her real property by paying off the outstanding lien plus penalties and other charges before a tax sale is referred to as a(n)
   a. equitable right of redemption.
   b. statutory right of redemption.
   c. redemption prior to foreclosure.
   d. equitable right of estoppel.

8. A public record listing the assessed value for all real property in the area is a(n)
   a. ad valorem file.
   b. assessment roll.
   c. local equalization roll.
   d. redemption file.

9. Who takes title to property through a tax foreclosure?
   a. The taxing body as lienholder
   b. The purchaser
   c. The purchaser, subject to the defaulted owner's statutory right of redemption
   d. The State of New York

ANSWER KEY

CHAPTER 1

1. **d** The salesperson's license must be renewed every two years.
2. **b** A salesperson must take a 45-hour course.
3. **b** A broker must be at least 19 years of age.
4. **b** The broker's license is renewed every two years.
5. **a** Gloria is an associate broker.
6. **d** New York resident broker's principal place of business must be in New York.
7. **d** All documents must be kept on file for at least three years.
8. **a** Only a supervising broker may collect a commission.
9. **b** The name of the listing broker's firm must be included in any advertisement.
10. **c** Violations of the laws, rules, and regulations are misdemeanors.
11. **a** The correct term is commingling.
12. **d** Broker blind ads are prohibited.
13. **a** Reciprocal licensing requires the salesman to be licensed with a broker who has recropricity with that state.

CHAPTER 2

1. **c** A broker who represents a buyer is the buyer's agent.
2. **b** A salesperson is the broker's agent and seller's subagent.
3. **b** Agency is representing a principal in one specific transaction under detailed instructions.
4. **b** Dual agency is permissible when the informed consent of all parties has been given.
5. **c** Representing two principals in the same transaction is dual agency.
6. **c** Entering into an agency agreement is not a characteristic of a ready, willing, and able buyer.
7. **b** Betty is self-dealing.
8. **d** The statement defines a universal agent.
9. **d** Sam is engaging in puffing: statements of opinion regarding the qualities of a property.
10. **a** The statement defines a special agent.
11. **b** Compensation is always mutually negotiable.
12. **d** A salesperson is compensated by only the broker.

CHAPTER 3

1. **c** Net listings are illegal in New York.
2. **a** A single agent represents either a buyer or a seller.
3. **d** Listing agents should always obtain the informed consent of the seller prior to entering into a cooperative agreement that creates a subagency.
4. **c** Agents must disclose and obtain signed acknowledgments of their agency relationships at the time of the first substantive contact with a party.
5. **b** A buyer agent may be compensated by either the buyer or the seller.

6. **c** The statement defines a simple offer of cooperation.
7. **b** An exclusive right to represent is the most common form of buyer agency.
8. **b** The example illustrates circumstances that may give rise to undisclosed dual agency situations.
9. **a** An open listing offers a broker the least protection, because it applies the fewest restrictions on the seller.
10. **c** The example defines disclosed dual agency.
11. **b** The buyer's financial condition is a material fact needed by the seller.
12. **a** A broker and his agents are required to perform due diligence.
13. **d** First substantive contact occurs when the buyer walks into the agent's office and begins to discuss his or her needs or financial situation.

CHAPTER 4

1. **c** The statement defines real property.
2. **b** The surface and sub-surface rights to property may be held by different owners.
3. **d** An owner has riparian rights to the middle of a nonnavigable waterway.
4. **a** The statement defines a trade fixture.
5. **d** Severalty of ownership is sole ownership.
6. **c** The four unities (time, title, interest, and possession) are required in a joint tenancy.

7. **b** The statement defines tenancy by the entirety; NY is not a community property state.

8. **a** The statement defines a type of syndicate.

9. **b** The statement defines cooperative ownership.

10. **c** The statement is an example of chattels.

CHAPTER 5

1. **b** A judgment becomes a lien when it is docketed.

2. **c** A vendor's lien is a seller's claim against a purchaser who has not paid.

3. **b** The dominant tenement is benefited.

4. **d** The statement defines license.

5. **d** Personal attachment is an element of an easment in gross.

6. **b** The statement is an example of an encroachment.

7. **a** The statement defines easement by prescription.

8. **c** The facts describe a subordination agreement.

9. **c** Estate and inheritance taxes are on the property of a deceased owner.

10. **a** The statement describes a mechanic's lien.

CHAPTER 6

1. **b** A metes-and-bounds description uses monuments and a point of beginning.

2. **c** A referee's deed contains no covenants or warrantees.

3. **d** The Geodetic Survey is used to compute vertical elevations.

4. **d** The law of intestacy governs property of a person who dies without leaving a will.

5. **d** Recital of warranties and covenants is not necessary to a valid deed.

6. **a** A general warranty deed offers the most protection.

7. **d** The statement defines special warranty deed.

8. **c** A quitclaim deed provides the least protection.

9. **d** There are 640 acres in one square mile.

10. **c** A bargain and sale deed carries no warranties, but implies grantor holds title.

CHAPTER 7

1. **b** A periodic lease runs for an indefinite period.

2. **c** Only leases for more than one year must be in writing.

3. **a** An oral lease is valid if it is for a term of less than one year.

4. **d** The security deposit requirement applies only to owners of six or more units.

5. **a** A tenant's death does not terminate his or her lease.

6. **c** The statement defines actual eviction.

7. **b** The example illustrates a periodic lease.

8. **a** The statement defines a gross lease.

9. **c** The statement defines a percentage lease.

10. **b** The example illustrates a net lease.

CHAPTER 8

1. **c** The statement defines unilateral contract.

2. **c** The substitution of a new contract for an existing one is novation.

3. **c** The New York statute of limitations for contract actions is six years.

4. **b** The statement defines a land contract.

5. **b** The statute of frauds requires a writing for certain types of contracts.

6. **d** Specific performance is a legal action to compel compliance with a contract.

7. **d** While consideration is an essential element of a contract, it does not have to be monetary.

8. **c** The statement defines an unenforceable contract.

9. **a** The statement defines a void contract.

10. **b** The statement defines a voidable contract.

CHAPTER 9

1. **b** Actual notice is real knowledge obtained by firsthand observation.

2. **c** HUD Form 1 is not evidence of title.

3. **d** A coinsurance clause requires 80 percent of replacement cost.

4. **a** The statement defines an abstract of title.

5. **b** Recording documents gives constructive notice to the world.

6. **a** The statement defines credit.

7. **d** The statement defines a proration.

8. **c** RESPA requires disclosure; the Uniform Settlement Statement is the tool for disclosing.

9. **c** The statement defines a closing statement.

10. **b** The statement defines debit.

CHAPTER 10

1. **c** The mortgagor is the borrower.
2. **a** The mortgagee is a lender.
3. **d** Recording the release will clear a mortgage lien.
4. **c** In New York, the statutory usury ceiling floats, and is adjusted periodically.
5. **d** Loans greater than $2.5 million are exempt.
6. **b** The statement defines point.
7. **a** A subsequent owner is personally liable when he or she assumes a loan.
8. **a** The statement defines an adjustable-rate mortgage (ARM).
9. **a** NY is a lien theory state.
10. **b** The statement defines. loan-to-value ratio (LTV).

CHAPTER 11

1. **c** The statement defines cap.
2. **b** The statement defines ceiling.
3. **a** The statement defines margin.
4. **c** ECOA is the Equal Credit Opportunity Act.
5. **d** The statement defines Regulation Z.
6. **c** The statement defines a bridge loan.
7. **b** The statement defines Fannie Mae.
8. **c** A takeout loan is used in construction projects.
9. **d** The statement defines negative amortization.
10. **d** The statement defines a sale-and-leaseback agreement.

CHAPTER 12

1. **b** Recording a deed is a private land-use control.
2. **c** Taxation and escheat are public land-use controls.
3. **b** The issues would be regulated by building codes.
4. **a** The statement defines zoning ordinances.
5. **d** Escheat is unrelated to zoning issues.
6. **c** The statement defines certificate of occupancy.
7. **b** Condemnation is the method by which eminent domain is exercised.
8. **a** The scenario is spot zoning; nonharmonious uses are illegal in NY.
9. **a** The statement defines police power.
10. **b** The statement defines nonconforming use.

CHAPTER 13

1. **d** Gussets are in a truss roof.
2. **b** The statement defines balloon framing.
3. **b** The statement defines slider windows.
4. **c** Jalousie and casement windows use gears.
5. **c** Hollow core doors are interior only.
6. **c** The NY Home Improvement Law applies to purchases over $500.
7. **b** The systems warranty lasts for two years.
8. **a** The materials warranty lasts for one year.
9. **d** The structural defects warranty is six years.
10. **c** Higher R-value = more resistance.

CHAPTER 14

1. **c** Indestructibility is a physical characteristic.
2. **d** The statement defines value.

3. **b** The statement defines market value.
4. **d** Regression refers to a negative effect of one property's value on neighboring home prices.
5. **a** The statement defines the cost approach.
6. **c** Rents are used in the income capitalization approach.
7. **b** The statement defines depreciation.
8. **d** The property suffers from functional obsolescence.
9. **c** The example describes physical deterioration.
10. **c** The statement defines CMA.

CHAPTER 15

1. **b** Sexual orientation is protected by some local laws, but not federal law.
2. **d** There are no exemptions for brokers.
3. **d** There are no exemptions for race.
4. **d** Fine is $25,000 for a second violation in five years.
5. **c** Fine is $50,000 for three or more violations in seven years.
6. **d** There is no limit under the Civil Rights Act.
7. **c** The statement defines affirmative marketing.
8. **a** The statement defines blockbusting.

CHAPTER 16

1. **c** Asbestos is hazardous as dust and fibers.
2. **c** Paint, plumbing pipes, and airborne particles are a common source of lead contamination.
3. **b** Owners are not required to test for lead.

4. **b** Contamination is confirmed in Phase II.

5. **d** Superfund liability is joint and several, strict, and retroactive.

6. **a** Due diligence is the responsibility of all the professionals involved in the transaction.

7. **a** The statement defines percolation.

8. **c** The statement defines pollution.

9. **b** The statement describes the symptoms of lead poisoning.

10. **a** The statement describes PCBs.

CHAPTER 17

1. **c** **$1,194.00 total cost**
   4" ÷ 12 = 0.333'
   Concrete: 40' × 15' × 0.333 = 199.8 Cubic Feet ÷ 27 = 7.4 Cubic Yards × $60 per Cubic Yard = $444
   Labor: 40' x 15' = 600 Square Feet × $1.25 per Square Foot = $750
   $444 Concrete + $750 Labor = $1,194.00 Total Cost

2. **b** **30%**
   $525 Monthly Rent × 12 Months = $6,300 Annual Rent ÷ $6,300 Annual Rent ÷ $21,000 = 0.3 or 30%

3. **a** **10,626.63 square feet**
   6" ÷ 12 = 0.5' + 75' = 75.5' Frontage
   9" ÷ 12 = 0.75' + 140 = 140.75' Depth
   140.75' × 75.5' = 10,626.63 Square Feet

4. **b** **$1,404 salesperson's commission**
   $58,500 sales price × 6% (or 0.06) = $3,510 full commission x 40% (or 0.4) = $1,404

5. **b** **9% annual interest rate**
   $450 × 2 = $900 Annual Interest
   $900 Annual Interest ÷ $10,000 Loan = 0.09 or 9%

6. **d** **117,600 cubic feet**
   120' × 80' = 9,600 Square Feet in Building – 1,200 Square Feet for Office = 8,400 Square Feet Left in Warehouse × 14" Ceiling = 117,600 Cubic Feet Left in Warehouse

7. **b** **$80,000 sales price**
   $5,200 Full Commission ÷ 6.5% (or 0.065) = $80,000 Sales Price

8. **d** **$310,000 sales price**
   $121,600 Seller's Net + $31,000 Closing Costs + $135,700 Loan Payoff = $288,300 Net after Commission
   100% Sales Price – 7% Commission = 93% Net after Commission
   $288,300 Net after Commission ÷ 93% (or 0.93) = $310,000 Sales Price

9. **c** **940 running feet**
   125' + 350' + 125' + 350' – 10' Gate = 940 Running Feet

10. **c** **$51.75 per front foot**
    $6,468.75 Price ÷ 125 Front Feet = $51.75 per Front Foot

CHAPTER 18

1. **c** Antitrust laws prohibit competing brokers from setting commission rates.

2. **d** The number of hours worked is irrelevant.

3. **d** A broker may provide office space for an independent contractor.

4. **d** The safe-harbor guidelines source of income, contract, and licensure.

5. **d** An independent contractor's compensation is usually performance-based.

6. **d** The licensee may work any hours he or she chooses.

7. **c** The employment contract, should be renewed each year.

8. **a** Illegal price-fixing occurs when competing brokers agree to set commission rates.

9. **b** Allocation of market occurs when competing firms agree to refrain from doing business in each other's territories.

10. **a** An independent contractor must comply with the broker's policy.

CHAPTER 19

1. **c** Antitrust laws prohibit competing brokers from setting commission rates.

2. **d** The number of hours worked is irrelevant.

3. **c** An MLS may charge a reasonable membership fee that is related to costs.

4. **a** The statement defines tie-in arrangement.

5. **d** An independent contractor's compensation is usually performance-based.

6. **a** The statement defines the purpose of a policy and procedures guide.

7. **c** Fair employment laws prevent employers from hir-

ing and firing without regard to performance.

8. **d** The GRI designation is awarded by the NY State Association of REALTORS®.

9. **b** The statement defines restraint of trade.

10. **a** Vicarious liability is created by the relationship between the parties.

CHAPTER 20

1. **c** The statement defines lien theory.

2. **b** A purchase-money mortgage is most commonly used for first-time purchases.

3. **d** A home-equity loan is a second mortgage taken on a homeowner's paid-up equity in the property.

4. **b** Blanket mortgages include more than one property.

5. **a** Package loans include both real and personal property.

6. **c** Construction loans are short-term and temporary.

7. **a** Cosntruction loan payments are made periodically.

8. **c** The statement defines sale-leaseback.

9. **b** An increase in interest and unemployment rates will cause real estate market activity to slow.

10. **b** The Fed's decisions affecting interest rates have a direct impact on the real estate market.

CHAPTER 21

1. **a** Low liquidity is a disadvantage.

2. **c** GRI − OE − DS = Cash Flow.

3. **b** A pro forma is a predictor.

4. **d** The formula describes adjusted basis.

5. **a** The statement defines basis.

6. **b** The statement defines boot.

7. **b** The statement defines cash flow.

8. **d** The statement defines general partnership.

9. **c** The statement defines limited liability company.

10. **a** REMIC was created by TRA 1986.

CHAPTER 22

1. **d** Ordinances are laws enacted by local communities.

2. **b** "Negotiable" means commercial paper may be transferred from one person to another by endorsement.

3. **c** Approval by the secretary of state is necessary for a corporation's certificate of incorporation.

4. **b** The statement defines a corporation.

5. **c** The statement defines a partnership.

6. **b or d** Organization such as an LLC or S corporation can achieve limited liability and avoid dual taxation.

7. **c** The federal court system is divided into four basic types of courts.

8. **c** There are four federal district courts in New York.

9. **d** In New York, the Court of Appeals is the highest court in the state.

10. **b** Criminal law governs injuries against society or the state.

CHAPTER 23

1. **c** The statement defines subdivider.

2. **b** The gridiron pattern is based on the government survey system.

3. **c** ILSFDA applies to 25 or more unit transactions.

4. **b** DOS regulates installment sales of subdivided land

5. **a** The statement defines condominium.

6. **c** At least 51 percent of tenants must intend to purchase.

7. **b** Purchasers have a 10-day right of rescission.

8. **d** The statement defines conversion.

9. **c** The statement defines a wetland survey.

10. **a** A proprietary lease is characteristic of a cooperative.

CHAPTER 24

1. **b** The statement defines title.

2. **c** The statement defines avulsion.

3. **c** The statement defines devisee.

4. **b** Both terms are forms of involuntary alienation.

5. **b** Adverse possession period is 10 years.

6. **d** An intestate's property escheats to the state if there are no heirs.

7. **c** A criminal record is irrelevant to will-making.

8. **a** The broker must be certain the client is the actual executor.

9. **c** The statement defines executor.

10. **b** The statement defines voluntary alienation.

CHAPTER 25

1. **b** A property manager is usual a general agent.
2. **c** Business interruption insurance replaces incom.
3. **c** Rent control regulations apply to 3+ unit properties built pre-2/47.
4. **a** Casualty insurance covers theft and vandalism.
5. **c** Rent stabilization applies to buildings of six or more units built between 2/47 and 1/1/71.

6. **c** Liability insurance covers injury to the public.
7. **b** The contract is a management agreement.
8. **b** The statement defines neighborhood analysis.
9. **d** ETPA includes rent stabilization.
10. **b** The statement defines surety.

CHAPTER 26

1. **c** The statement defines special assessment.
2. **d** The exemption age is 65.

3. **b** The statement defines a tax foreclosure.
4. **b** The statement defines statutory right of redemption.
5. **a** Ad valorem means 'according to value'.
6. **c** 1 mill = 1/10th of a cent.
7. **a** The statement defines the equitable right of redemption.
8. **b** The statement defines assessment roll.
9. **a** The taxing body/lienholder takes title 120.

APPENDIX: PREPARING FOR THE REAL ESTATE LICENSE EXAM

■ TEST-TAKING STRATEGIES

There are as many different ways to prepare for and take multiple-choice examinations as there are test-takers. Before you sit for the licensing exam, take some time to read this brief overview of test-taking strategies. While no one can tell you which method will work best for you, it's always a good idea to think about what you're going to do before you do it.

One of the most important things to remember about multiple-choice test questions is obvious: they always give you the correct answer. You don't have to remember how things are spelled, and you don't have to try to guess what the question is about. The answer is always there, right in front of you.

Of course, if it were as easy as that, it wouldn't be much of a test. The key to success in taking a multiple-choice examination is actually two keys:

1. **Know the correct answer.** You do that by going to class, paying attention, taking good notes, and studying the material. If you don't know the correct answer, be able to analyze the questions and answers effectively, so you can apply the second key, which is:
2. **Be able to make a reasonable guess.** Even if you don't know the answer, you will probably know which answers are clearly wrong, and which ones are more likely than the others to be right. If you can eliminate one answer as wrong, you have improved your odds of 'correct guessing' by 25 percent. Of course, if you can eliminate three wrong answers, your chance of a correct response is 100 percent.

There is no secret formula. The only sure way to improve your odds of a correct answer is to study and learn the material.

Structure of the Question

A multiple choice question has a basic structure. It starts with what test writers call the stem. That's the text of the question that sets up the need for an answer. The stem may be an incomplete statement that is finished by the correct answer; it may be a story problem or hypothetical example (called a **fact-pattern**). The stem is always followed by **options:** four possible answers to the question presented by the stem. The options may be single words or numbers, phrases, or complete sentences. Three of the options are **distractors.** These are the incorrect answers intended to 'distract' you from the correct answer, called the **key.**

Reading the Question

Here are three suggestions for how to read a multiple choice test question:

The Traditional Method. Read the question through from start to finish, then read the options. When you get to the correct answer, mark it and move on. This method works best for the type of short questions found on the New York exam, such as those that require completion or simply define a term. For longer, more complicated questions, however, you may miss important information.

The Focus Method. As we've seen, multiple choice questions have different parts. In all questions, the end of the stem will contain the question's *focus:* the basic issue the item asks you to address. That is, *the questions you must answer is usually in the last line or last few words of the stem.* In the focus method, read the end of the stem first. This will clue you in to what the question is about. Then go back and read the stem from beginning to end. You can watch for important items, and disregard unnecessary information. If you check for the question's focus first, you'll spot the test-writer's tricks.

For example, a long item about several characters might end like this: "Based on these facts, what type of agent is Broker Betty? By reading the last line first, you know to watch closely for agency issues in the fact pattern. Otherwise, you might waste time looking for fair housing or other brokerage issues.

The Upside-Down Method. This techniques takes the focus method one step further. Here, you do just what the name implies: you start reading the question from the bottom up. By reading the four options first, you can learn exactly what the test wants you to focus on.

Remember. The only certain way to pass the real estate exam is to **study.** Establish a schedule and stick to it. Read the assignments, answer the review questions, and pay close attention to lectures and exercises. While it's important to study before the text, avoid putting yourself in the position of having to "cram" for the licensing exam: last-minute panic won't help you pass and is a poor way to start off a career.

The Usual Advice

- Get a good night's rest—don't stay up late the night before the test trying to cram information into your brain.
- Don't rely on artificial stimulants (like coffee, caffeinated soft drinks, or sugar) to "perk you up" or make you sharper—the effect may actually be quite the opposite.
- Eat a good meal before the test.
- Wear comfortable clothes, including something you can put on if the room is cold, and something to take off it's not.
- Double-check before you leave for the test that you have all the things you'll need.
- Allow more than enough time to get to the testing location. Assume that traffic will be terrible, all the stoplights will be red, and all the trains or buses will be late.
- Try to relax—you'll work more efficiently and improve your concentration. Panic is not your friend.

Taking the License Exam

For best results, start by going through the entire examination, answering those questions you are certain about. By leaving the doubtful ones for last, you make sure you have time to mark all the answers you know are correct.

Once you've answered all the questions you feel sure about, return to the remaining questions. If you are unable to arrive at an answer the second time, make an educated guess. There is no penalty for guessing, so never leave a question unanswered.

If you've studied and learned the material well, don't worry—you have nothing to worry about. You *can* pass the exam, and go on to experience the excitement and success of a career in the rewarding field of real estate.

SALESPERSON'S PRACTICE EXAM I

1. A salesperson can legally accept a commission from whom?
   a. Another salesperson working for the same broker
   b. A property owner whose property is listed with the firm
   c. Any licensed broker
   d. His or her supervising broker

2. Which of the following must have a real estate license?
   a. A guardian acting under a court order
   b. A county administrator selling county owned property
   c. A resident manager who regularly rents vacated units
   d. The spouse of a licensed broker who shows and sells property of others to aid his or her spouse

3. A real estate salesperson must
   a. be at least 21 years of age.
   b. have completed 240 hours of instruction.
   c. have a sponsoring broker.
   d. have been a resident of New York for at least 2 years.

4. All of the following are required of a broker, *EXCEPT*
   a. display the licenses of all salespersons.
   b. prominently display his or her broker's license.
   c. notify the department of a change in business address.
   d. maintain a principal place of business.

5. A broker loaned money to a builder to complete a house, and the builder gave the broker an exclusive right to sell the home. The agency created in this relationship is
   a. general.
   b. universal.
   c. coupled with an interest.
   d. illegal.

6. A broker may collect a commission from both the buyer and seller in a transaction when
   a. both buyer and seller have prior knowledge of and consent to the arrangement.
   b. the total commission is not excessive
   c. the listing is coupled with an interest.
   d. the broker is exclusively a seller's agent.

7. The person who employs a broker is a
   a. fiduciary.
   b. principal.
   c. subagent.
   d. facilitator.

8. Which of the following may a broker properly do?
   a. Share a commission with another broker
   b. Give $100 gifts to friends for referrals
   c. Kick back a portion of a commission to a buyer
   d. Pay a finder's fee for a successful lead

9. Broker Mary lends a contractor the down payment for a special home. She will list the home when it is complete. This tie in is called
   a. buyer agency.
   b. agency coupled with interest.
   c. special agency.
   d. unbundling.

10. What is the result when a buyer client purchases a home listed in-house?
    a. No disclosure is required.
    b. The salesperson is not entitled to compensation.
    c. A dual agency is created.
    d. The transfer is unlawful.

11. A salesperson could avoid a dual agency in selling an in-house listing by
    a. informing the buyer that he or she is acting as a seller's agent.
    b. avoiding any mention of agency.
    c. acting as a buyer's agent.
    d. telling the purchaser that he or she will see that they get the best deal possible.

12. Co-ownership that automatically passes to the surviving co-owners upon the death of one co-owner is a
    a. tenancy-in-common.
    b. joint tenancy.
    c. corporate ownership.
    d. syndicate ownership.

13. All the following are legal tests of a fixture, *EXCEPT*
    a. adaptation to the real estate.
    b. cost of the item.
    c. intention and relationship of the parties.
    d. method of attachment.

14. Which of the following liens would be considered a general lien?
    a. Judgment lien
    b. Mechanic's lien
    c. Ad valorem taxes
    d. Mortgage lien

15. Mrs. Murphy has the right to cross over Mr. Green's property to gain access to her home. Mrs. Murphy has a(n)
    a. servient estate.
    b. easement in gross.
    c. dominant estate.
    d. license.

16. A valid deed requires all of the following, *EXCEPT*
    a. granting clause.
    b. recital of consideration.
    c. grantor who has reached the age of 21.
    d. an adequate description of the property.

17. Without acknowledgement, a deed cannot be
    a. delivered.
    b. recorded.
    c. valid.
    d. signed.

18. A lease for a definite period of time is a(n)
    a. periodic tenancy.
    b. estate for years.
    c. tenancy at will.
    d. tenancy at sufferance.

19. A written contract in which a buyer agrees to buy and a seller agrees to sell, with the sale to be completed at a definite date in the future would be
    a. express, bilateral, and executory.
    b. express, unilateral, and executory.
    c. express bilateral, and executed.
    d. implied, unilateral, and executed.

20. The substitution of a new contract for an existing one is a(n)
    a. assignment.
    b. breach.
    c. novation.
    d. unilateral contract.

21. A history of the recorded instruments affecting a property would be found in the
    a. deed.
    b. title policy.
    c. certificate of title.
    d. abstract.

22. In New York, a mortgage is a
    a. promise to pay a debt.
    b. lien on real property.
    c. the transfer of title to a lender.
    d. the transfer of title to a trustee.

23. A buyer of property who is NOT personally obligated to pay the mortgage debt would most likely have purchased the property
    a. with a subordination agreement.
    b. and assumed the mortgage.
    c. subject to the mortgage.
    d. with an estoppel certificate.

24. An assumable mortgage would have all of the following, *EXCEPT* a(n)
    a. alienation clause.
    b. acceleration clause.
    c. subordination agreement.
    d. mortgage note.

25. The illegal practice of charging more than the maximum permitted interest rate is
    a. "buydown."   c. usury.
    b. alienation.   d. acceleration.

26. A mortgage broker is
    a. one who assists with credit restoration.
    b. one who for a fee, acts as an intermediary between the lender and borrower.
    c. the lender in a real estate transaction.
    d. sets the mortgage rates.

27. In order to obtain a zoning variance a property, owner must show that the zoning
    a. creates an unnecessary hardship.
    b. does not comply with the master plan.
    c. is not in conformance with private restrictions.
    d. variance is needed for the public good.

28. After proper completion of a new building, the building inspector issues a certificate of
    a. use.   c. variance.
    b. occupancy.   d. permission.

29. Vertical building frame wall members that are spaced at even intervals and rest upon a plate are
    a. studs.   c. headers.
    b. rafters.   d. fire stops.

30. R value relates to which of the following?
    a. The angle of a pitched roof
    b. The insulation factor of a material
    c. The tensile strength of a truss
    d. The efficiency of a septic system

31. Market value is defined as
    a. the price actually paid for a property.
    b. the most likely price obtainable in a free, open, and informed market.
    c. the cost to an owner including improvements.
    d. the maximum value a property can be insured for.

32. An appraiser interested in the present value of future income would use which approach to value?
    a. Market analysis
    b. Cost approach
    c. Income-capitalization
    d. Direct sales comparison

33. Inducing an owner to sell because persons of a different race are entering the neighborhood is
    a. steering.   c. redlining.
    b. white flight.   d. blockbusting.

34. The 1968 U.S. Supreme Court case of *Jones v. Alfred H. Mayer Company* upheld
    a. the Civil Rights Act of 1866.
    b. the Civil Rights Act of 1968.
    c. redlining.
    d. subsidized housing for the poor.

35. Directing white prospective homebuyers away from racially mixed areas is
    a. blockbusting.   c. steering.
    b. redlining.   d. apportionment.

36. A lender's refusal to make loans in a specified area without regard to the economic qualifications of loan applicants would be
    a. legal.   c. blockbusting.
    b. redlining.   d. steering.

37. Which of the following might be excused from Superfund liability?
    a. A former owner who did not understand the hazard
    b. A transporter of the hazardous waste
    c. A lender who acquired by foreclosure
    d. A person who unintentionally polluted

38. If seven former owners were responsible for hazardous waste on a site, each one could be held liable for
    a. ⅐th of the clean-up costs only.
    b. the entire damage.
    c. only for damage relating to negligence.
    d. only for the damage that can be related to that person.

39. A real estate license, once issued, is good for how many years?
- **a.** One
- **b.** Two
- **c.** Three
- **d.** Four

40. A type of contract in which an owner must sell but the buyer is not required to buy is a(n)
- **a.** open offer.
- **b.** land contract.
- **c.** option.
- **d.** listing.

41. Sloping timbers that support the roof are called
- **a.** collar beams.
- **b.** b. ridge boards.
- **c.** rafters.
- **d.** ceiling joists.

42. Grandma will give her home to her grandson Josh, but her daughter is allowed to stay in the home till she dies. This is called
- **a.** tenancy in the entirety.
- **b.** tenancy at will.
- **c.** life tenancy.
- **d.** joint tenancy.

43. All of the following are acceptable legal descriptions of property, *EXCEPT* a
- **a.** description based on a government survey.
- **b.** PO address.
- **c.** reference to a recorded plot map.
- **d.** metes and bounds description.

44. A valid real estate contract requires all of the following, *EXCEPT*
- **a.** a signed writing.
- **b.** competent parties.
- **c.** notarized.
- **d.** offer and acceptance.

45. When showing buyer/customers her listing, Sue promised to "get this home at the price you want to pay." She has now entered into what relationship?
- **a.** Self-dealing
- **b.** Fraud
- **c.** Procuring cause
- **d.** Undisclosed dual agency

46. It would be legal for a broker to
- **a.** require a builder who buys a lot to agree to list the completed house with the broker.
- **b.** agree with other brokers not to cooperate with another broker.
- **c.** set minimum commissions with other brokers.
- **d.** set a commissions schedule for his or her office without regard to fees charged by others.

47. When a mortgage is paid in full, the
- **a.** mortgagor gives the mortgagee a release.
- **b.** mortgagee gives the mortgagor a satisfaction of mortgage.
- **c.** trustee returns legal title to the beneficiary.
- **d.** mortgage would now be recorded.

48. The government may take private property for public use under which power?
- **a.** Escheat
- **b.** Police
- **c.** taxation
- **d.** Eminent domain

49. A person who believes that he or she was discriminated against in housing may file a charge with which government agency?
- **a.** HUD
- **b.** FHA
- **c.** FBI
- **d.** FCC

50. A good faith estimate of settlement costs is required by
- **a.** a title insurer.
- **b.** RESPA.
- **c.** Truth-In-Lending Act.
- **d.** DOS.

SALESPERSON'S PRACTICE EXAM II

1. What must a broker do when he or she receives a purchase offer?
   a. Immediately file it with the state
   b. Promptly present it to the owner of the property
   c. Keep a copy on file for 10 years
   d. Retain it for 7 days to allow the presentation of competing offers

2. A blind ad is an ad that fails to include
   a. the property's address.
   b. the owner's name.
   c. an indication that the person placing the ad is a broker.
   d. the broker's telephone number.

3. All of the following are violations of the license law, *EXCEPT*
   a. acting for more than one party to a transaction without the knowledge and consent of all parties.
   b. a broker sharing a commission with another broker.
   c. failing to remit monies belonging to others within a reasonable period of time.
   d. making a material misstatement in a license application.

4. A person authorized to represent a principal in the sale of a particular property is a(n)
   a. universal agent.   c. intended agent.
   b. general agent.   d. special agent.

5. What should a broker do when his agent wishes to purchase an office listing?
   a. Present the offer immediately
   b. Sever the listing agreement to avoid conflict of interest
   c. Forbid the sale
   d. Ask the seller to sign a dual agency form

6. An express agreement used to create an agency between a broker and an owner is a(n)
   a. subagency agreement.
   b. listing agreement.
   c. implied agency contract.
   d. procuring cause stipulation.

7. In addition to being the agent of his or her broker, a salesperson
   a. is the general agent of the principal.
   b. has no fiduciary responsibilities.
   c. is a subagent of the principal.
   d. is the designated agent of the principal.

8. Which of the following acts may properly be performed by a real estate salesperson?
   a. Sell his or her own property (providing the buyer is informed of the salesperson's interest)
   b. Refuse to accept any offer of which he or she disapproves
   c. Accept a commission directly from a principal
   d. Misrepresent a property if done so at the direction of the principal

9. By accepting the terms of an unauthorized lease negotiated by a broker, the owner created a(n)
   a. express agency.   c. dual agency.
   b. agency by ratification.   d. universal agency.

10. A listing that could be simultaneously given to more than one broker would be a(n)
    a. exclusive agency listing.
    b. exclusive right-to-sell listing.
    c. open listing.
    d. net listing.

11. A listing where the owner does not owe a commission if the owner procures a buyer without agency help is what type of listing?
    a. Multiple
    b. Exclusive right-to-sell
    c. Net
    d. Exclusive agency

12. Albert, Baker, Charley, and Doris are joint tenants. Albert dies and then Baker sells to Edith. The result would be
    a. Albert's heirs, Charley, Doris, and Edith are tenants in common.
    b. Charley, Doris, and Edith are joint tenants.
    c. Charley, Doris, and Edith are tenants in common.
    d. Charley and Doris are joint tenants and Edith is a tenant in common.

13. An easement by prescription can be acquired in New York after use of property belonging to another for how many years?
    a. 1   c. 25
    b. 10   d. 99

14. What type of deed transfers only the owner's interest, making no warranties or claims of ownership?
    a. Trustee's   c. Executor's
    b. Warranty   d. Quitclaim

15. A tenancy that automatically terminates upon the death of either the landlord or tenant is a(n)
    a. tenancy at sufferance.
    b. estate for years.
    c. tenancy at will.
    d. month-to-month tenancy.

16. A lease in which the lessee pays a fixed rental and the landlord pays the taxes and maintains the property is what kind of lease?
    a. Gross   c. Percentage
    b. Net   d. Triple-net

17. A seller refuses to honor a sales agreement for the sale of a home. The buyer, who wants the property, should ask the court for
    a. rescission.
    b. compensatory damages.
    c. specific performance.
    d. a novation.

18. All of the following would be a prorated expense in a real estate closing, EXCEPT
    a. broker's commission.
    b. property taxes paid in advance.
    c. accrued interest on an assumed loan.
    d. prepaid rents.

19. A three-day right of rescission for a consumer loan secured by the borrower's residence is provided for by
    a. New York's usury law.
    b. the Equal Credit Opportunity Act.
    c. Regulation Z.
    d. RESPA.

20. The Equal Credit Opportunity Act prohibits discrimination against credit applicants on the basis of all the following factors, EXCEPT
    a. source of income.
    b. poor credit history.
    c. marital status.
    d. race.

21. Which law requires that the annual percentage rate be included in ads that refer to loan terms?
    a. Real Estate Settlement Procedures Act
    b. Equal Credit Opportunity Act
    c. New York usury law
    d. Regulation Z

22. A lender who brings together borrowers and lenders is referred to as a(n)
    a. credit union.   c. mortgage broker.
    b. insurance company.   d. mortgage banker.

23. Which of the following would cause the loss of a nonconforming use?
    a. The owner fails to obtain a special use permit.
    b. The owner fails to change the zoning.
    c. The building was destroyed or torn down.
    d. The zoning ordinance is enacted into law.

24. Government land use controls include all of the following, *EXCEPT*
    a. environmental laws.   c. zoning.
    b. subdivision controls. d. deed restrictions.

25. A 220 volt line coming into a home means
    a. the property has been rewired.
    b. the panel box is up to code.
    c. each outlet can handle any appliance.
    d. that the voltage come to the panel box. How the volts are distributed needs further investigation.

26. The approach that would be most appropriate for a non-income producing service building would be the
    a. direct sales comparison approach.
    b. CMA.
    c. cost approach.
    d. income capitalization approach.

27. When preparing a CMA, what would not be considered important to the result?
    a. The original cost of the property
    b. The assessed valuation
    c. The seller's 'bottom line'
    d. The age of the property

28. A real estate advertisement may include which of the following statements?
    a. "French buyers are preferred."
    b. "No wheelchairs or guide dogs, please."
    c. "Families with children preferred."
    d. "Say 'Merry Christmas' with a new house!"

29. A landlord might legally refuse to rent to which of the following tenants?
    a. A visually impaired person who has a guide dog when the landlord has a strict "no pets" policy
    b. A drug addict
    c. A person who has a mentally ill spouse
    d. A prospective tenant who has children, when all other tenants are 62 or older

30. The Civil Rights Act of 1866 prohibits discrimination based on
    a. familial status.   c. race.
    b. handicap.   d. gender.

31. A naturally-occurring substance most often found concentrated in poorly-ventilated areas is
    a. asbestos.   c. CFCs.
    b. radon gas.   d. PCBs.

32. The size requirement of a septic tank would be determined by which of the following factors?
    a. The number of bedrooms in the house
    b. The average age of the residents
    c. The total square footage of the lot
    d. The total square footage of the house

33. An example of personal property would be
    a. firewood.
    b. a concrete walk.
    c. a vacant lot.
    d. ornamental landscaping.

34. Buyer credits on a closing statement would NOT include
    a. the earnest money paid.
    b. a loan balance being assumed.
    c. a new mortgage given to the seller.
    d. commission paid by the seller.

35. Littoral rights refer to
    a. rights to use a river or stream.
    b. air rights.
    c. rights to use nonflowing water bordering a property.
    d. tenant rights in trade fixtures.

36. Which of the following is a general lien?
    a. Judgment lien
    b. Mechanic's lien
    c. Tax lien
    d. Mortgage

37. A lease that automatically renews for similar succeeding periods creates a tenancy
    a. at will.
    b. periodic.
    c. at sufferance.
    d. for years.

38. An unlicensed real estate assistant may perform all of the following activities, *EXCEPT*
    a. type contracts for broker approval.
    b. place or remove signs on property.
    c. negotiate real estate transactions.
    d. compute commission checks.

39. From an owner's point of view, the least restrictive type of listing would be a(n)
    a. net listing.
    b. open listing.
    c. exclusive right-to-sell listing.
    d. exclusive agency listing.

40. A 3,000 square foot home with only one bath is most likely an example of which type of obsolescence?
    a. Locational
    b. Economic
    c. Functional
    d. Deteriorative

41. If a foreclosure sale fails to produce sufficient funds to repay a mortgage debt, the defaulted mortgagor may be subject to a(n)
    a. deficiency judgment.
    b. estoppel order.
    c. balloon payment.
    d. satisfaction lien.

42. The overhang of a pitched roof that extends beyond the exterior walls of a house is the
    a. pier.
    b. facia.
    c. eaves.
    d. ridge board.

43. What is a primary source of lead poisoning?
    a. Gases released from rocks
    b. Foam-type insulation
    c. Paint and plumbing
    d. Decomposition of asbestos

44. Which of the following would NOT be considered real property?
    a. Trade fixtures
    b. Land
    c. Permanent improvements to land
    d. Growing trees

45. The most complete form of real estate ownership is a(n)
    a. life estate.
    b. fee on condition.
    c. estate at will.
    d. fee simple.

46. Which of the following is NOT a requirement of agency relationships?
    a. The agent must exercise care.
    b. The agent must receive compensation.
    c. The agent must obey the principal's legal instructions.
    d. The agent must disclose to the principal any facts that could affect the principal's decisions.

47. A right to use property that is created by the actual use of the property is a(n)
    a. easement by necessity.
    b. easement by prescription.
    c. license.
    d. lis pendens.

48. Which of the following is true regarding the rectangular (government) survey system?
    a. There are 160 sections in a township.
    b. A section is 6 miles square.
    c. There are 36 square miles in a section.
    d. There are 640 acres in a section.

49. Which of the following events would terminate a lease?
  a. Lessor's death
  b. Lessee's death
  c. Destruction of the property
  d. Sale of the premises

50. A contract in which neither party can force the other to perform, but which can be treated by both parties as a good contract, is
  a. void.   **c.** voidable.
  b. valid.   **d.** unenforceable.

51. A real estate advertisement may not include the following statement.
  a. Handicapped accessible.
  b. No children.
  c. Gated community.
  d. Walk to worship.

ANSWER KEY FOR SALESPERSON'S PRACTICE EXAMS

with chapter references to *Modern Real Estate Practice in New York*, 8th Edition

PRACTICE EXAM I

1. d 1
2. d 1
3. c 1
4. a 1
5. c 2
6. a 2
7. b 2
8. a 2
9. b 3
10. c 3
11. a 3
12. b 4
13. b 4
14. a 5
15. c 5
16. c 6
17. b 6
18. b 7
19. a 8
20. c 8
21. d 9
22. b 10
23. c 10
24. a 10
25. c 10
26. b 10
27. a 12
28. b 12
29. a 13
30. b 13
31. b 14
32. c 14
33. d 15
34. a 15

35. c 15
36. b 15
37. c 16
38. b 16
39. b 1
40. c 8
41. c 13
42. c 4
43. b 6
44. a 8
45. d 2
46. d 3
47. b 10
48. d 12
49. a 15
50. b 9

PRACTICE EXAM II

1. b 1
2. c 1
3. b 1
4. d 2
5. b 2
6. b 2
7. c 2
8. a 2
9. b 2
10. c 3
11. d 3
12. d 4
13. b 5
14. d 6
15. c 7
16. a 7
17. c 8

18. a 9
19. c 10
20. b 10
21. d 10
22. c 10
23. c 12
24. d 12
25. d 13
26. c 14
27. d 14
28. d 15
29. d 15
30. c 15
31. b 16
32. a 16
33. a 4
34. d 9
35. c 4
36. a 5
37. b 7
38. c 1
39. b 3
40. c 14
41. a 10
42. c 13
43. c 16
44. a 4
45. d 4
46. b 2
47. b 5
48. d 6
49. c 7
50. d 8
51. b 12

BROKER'S PRACTICE EXAM I

1. The minimum age for a broker in New York is
   a. 18.
   b. 19.
   c. 20.
   d. 21.

2. Nonresidents who are licensed as brokers in New York must do all of the following, *EXCEPT*
   a. pay license fees.
   b. maintain a place of business in the state.
   c. meet age eligibility requirements.
   d. obey New York disclosure laws.

3. An associate broker is
   a. a person who has passed a broker's exam but works as a salesperson under supervision of a sponsoring broker.
   b. a person who, while not licensed, has a licensed broker as his or her employee.
   c. a salesperson who has not yet passed his or her broker's examination.
   d. a person who, while licensed as a salesperson, does not work under a broker's supervision.

4. A listing in which the listing broker earns a commission no matter who procures the buyer is what type of listing'
   a. Open
   b. Exclusive agency
   c. Exclusive right to sell
   d. Buyer's

5. When the government exercises eminent domain, all the following are true, *EXCEPT*
   a. the proposed use must be a public use.
   b. just compensation must be paid to the owner.
   c. the owner must consent.
   d. the rights of the owner must be protected by due process of law.

6. Hypersensitivity, asthma, and allergies that persist when a person is away from a building may be symptoms of
   a. lead poisoning.
   b. sick building syndrome.
   c. EMF exposure.
   d. building-related illness.

7. An unlicensed real estate assistant may perform all the following acts, *EXCEPT*
   a. arrange appointments for a licensee.
   b. assemble documents for closing.
   c. negotiate a lease for a licensee.
   d. place For Sale signs on properties.

8. The federal law otherwise known as the Truth-in-Lending Act is
   a. RESPA.
   b. Regulation Z.
   c. ECOA.
   d. FHLMC.

9. A real estate broker who is to receive a sales commission as well as a mortgage broker commission for arranging the buyer's loan must do which of the following?
   a. Obtain the informed consent of all parties
   b. Remit the loan broker commission to the buyer
   c. Remit the loan broker commission to the seller
   d. Obtain DOS approval in order to accept both fees

10. Copies of agency disclosure forms obtained in the course of a broker's business must be kept for
    a. 90 days.
    b. 1 year.
    c. 3 years.
    d. 7 years.

11. When a broker acts as a buyer's agent in the sale of an in-house listing, the result would be
    a. an automatic violation of the law.
    b. dual agency.
    c. cancellation of the seller agency.
    d. that the buyer and seller would share equally in a single broker fee.

12. The duty owed to a seller by a buyer's agent is
    a. the same as that owed by a seller's agent.
    b. iduciary duty.
    c. one of loyalty, confidentiality and disclosure.
    d. one of fair play and honest dealing.

13. A group of brokers agree not to cooperate with another broker. This practice, which is prohibited by the antitrust laws, is known as
    a. market allocation.
    b. a tie-in arrangement.
    c. market fixing.
    d. group boycotting.

14. A broker sold a lot to a builder with the provision that the builder list the house with the broker. This agreement is
    a. a tie-in sale.
    b. legal under antitrust law.
    c. considered market allocation.
    d. a price fixing violation of the antitrust laws.

15. Before a septic system can be installed, which of the following tests must be performed?
    a. EMF   c. Contamination
    b. Radon   d. Percolation

16. A Registrar of Titles issues a certificate of title under the
    a. title insurance system.
    b. principle of caveat emptor.
    c. abstract system.
    d. torrens system.

17. A person who is not licensed as a broker may properly accept compensation for which of the following?
    a. Negotiating a loan secured by a mortgage
    b. Arranging an exchange of real property
    c. Handling rentals and rent collection as part of a resident manager's duties
    d. Selling real property by auction

18. A real estate broker authorized to locate a buyer for a particular property would be considered what type of agent?
    a. General   c. Universal
    b. Special   d. Independent

19. A commercial sale leaseback arrangement benefits the seller/lessee because it
    a. reduces monthly expenses.
    b. allows for tax benefits.
    c. provides for a guaranteed income.
    d. frees capital for operations.

20. If a seller offers to finance a loan at an artificially low rate of interest, the IRS may
    a. impute a higher rate for tax purposes.
    b. void the transaction.
    c. require that the seller triple the rate.
    d. invoke its power to accelerate the loan.

21. A loan in which the borrower receives regular monthly payments based on home equity is a(n)
    a. temporary loan.
    b. reverse annuity loan.
    c. shared-equity loan.
    d. wraparound mortgage.

22. A buyer who wishes to avoid liability for a mortgage debt would buy
    a. and assume an existing mortgage.
    b. using an alienation clause.
    c. using an acceleration clause.
    d. subject to the existing mortgage.

23. A disadvantage of accepting a deed in lieu of foreclosure is that
    a. the person receiving the deed would be liable for any deficiency judgement.
    b. the mortgagee takes the property subject to junior liens.
    c. it is more time consuming than the foreclosure process.
    d. the mortgagee gives up the right to any profit on a later sale.

24. An owner calls you to list his property and tells you his taxes are $3,000 including a veteran's exemption. When preparing the listing sheet for potential buyers, you treat the exemption as
   a. a selling point.
   b. check with the municipality for the exact taxes and report as such.
   c. ignore the exemption—that's a buyer's brokers responsibility.
   d. ignore the exemption—it will expire.

25. A loan in which the borrower receives a monthly check from the lender would be which of the following?
   a. Reverse annuity loan
   b. Shared-equity loan
   c. Package loan
   d. Wraparound mortgage

26. A point equals
   a. ¹⁄₁₀ of 1 percent of the sales price.
   b. 1 percent of the sales price.
   c. ¹⁄₁₀ of 1 percent of the loan amount.
   d. 1 percent of the loan amount.

27. A statement from a lender that details the amount remaining and currently due on a mortgage is referred to as a
   a. satisfaction of mortgage.
   b. alienation statement.
   c. reduction certificate.
   d. certificate of net present value.

28. Depreciation taken in equal installments over the asset's useful life is known as
   a. straight-line.   c. passive.
   b. ACRS.   d. marginal.

29. All the following are true of a 1031 exchange, *EXCEPT*
   a. properties must be of like kind.
   b. properties must be investment properties or properties used in trade or business.
   c. if boot is given, the the party receiving boot is taxed on it.
   d. a 1031 exchange is taxed as a sale at a special reduced rate.

30. Which lien would have priority over all other liens?
   a. Mortgage
   b. Mechanic's lien
   c. Real property tax lien
   d. Judgment lien

31. A person who has commenced a lawsuit that affects title to real estate can protect his or her interests by filing a(n)
   a. stop order.
   b. easement.
   c. lis pendens.
   d. notice of intent.

32. Investor Jones traded a lot to investor Smith. Smith gave Jones $10,000 to balance the trade. Based on these facts, which of the following statements is true?
   a. Jones will be taxed on the $10,000 boot.
   b. Neither Jones nor Smith have any tax liability in this Section 1031 exchange.
   c. Jones and Smith share the tax liability.
   d. Jones is entitled to a $10,000 tax credit.

33. A valid contract for the sale of real estate in New York requires all the following, *EXCEPT*
   a. adequate description.
   b. competent parties.
   c. signature of a witness.
   d. written contract.

34. A lease where the tenant pays the taxes, insurance, and all maintenance costs in addition to the rent would be a
   a. gross lease.   c. flat lease.
   b. percentage lease.   d. net lease.

35. A deed that makes no claim that the grantor has any interest in a property but conveys whatever interest the grantor has is a
   a. bargain and sale deed.
   b. quit claim deed.
   c. deed from a corporation.
   d. full warranty deed.

36. If a defaulted mortgagor refuses to leave the property after a foreclosure sale, he or she has a(n)
    a. periodic tenancy.
    b. tenancy at sufferance.
    c. tenancy at will.
    d. estate for years.

37. To protect an owner against injury claims of persons entering the premises, a property owner would want
    a. content insurance.
    b. fire and hazard insurance.
    c. liability insurance.
    d. a surety bond.

38. Which of the following is true regarding the rights and obligations of tenants and landlords?
    a. Tenants must maintain appliances furnished by the landlord.
    b. A landlord may enter without permission only in an emergency.
    c. Tenants have a legal duty to keep the building free of vermin.
    d. Tenants are responsible for smoke detectors.

39. To be valid in New York a deed must have all of the following EXCEPT a(n)
    a. acknowledgment.
    b. words of conveyance.
    c. competent grantor.
    d. adequate description of the real estate.

40. Which of the following correctly states the parol evidence rule?
    a. A later agreement takes priority over a prior agreement.
    b. Words take precedence over numerals.
    c. Contract ambiguities should be interpreted against the party drafting the agreement.
    d. Written contracts take precedence over oral agreements or promises.

41. Acquiring title to the land of another by continuous, open, notorious, and hostile use is known as
    a. adverse possession.
    b. tacking on.
    c. natural process.
    d. condemnation.

42. A transfer of title as a gift to the government is
    a. involuntary alienation.
    b. dedication.
    c. adverse possession.
    d. escheat.

43. Damages agreed to in advance by parties to a contract that serves as full compensation should one of the parties breach the agreement, are what type of damages?
    a. Compensatory   c. Liquidated
    b. Nominal   d. Punitive

44. A legal proceeding to divide a jointly owned property is
    a. adverse possession.   c. probate.
    b. foreclosure.   d. partition.

45. In New York, a surviving spouse is entitled to the greater of one-third of the estate or $50,000 plus what portion of the remainder of the estate?
    a. One-quarter   c. One-third
    b. One-half   d. Two-thirds

46. A development with rectangular blocks and lots is a pattern of development known as a
    a. gridiron.   c. radius.
    b. loop.   d. curvilinear.

47. An existing use that is allowed to continue when zoning is changed, even though the new zoning law precludes such a use, is known as a
    a. zoning variance.
    b. restrictive development.
    c. nonconforming use.
    d. deed restriction.

48. A restriction on land use placed by a subdivider rather than a governmental unit is referred to as
    a. adverse control.
    b. involuntary alienation.
    c. zoning.
    d. restrictive covenants.

49. The registration requirement of the Interstate Land Sales Full Disclosure Act applies to the sale or leasing of how many lots?
   a. 5 or more
   b. 25 or more
   c. 50 or more
   d. 100 or more

50. A property in which title to the land and building is held by a corporation, with each apartment purchaser receiving stock in the corporation as well as a proprietary lease for his or her apartment, is a
   a. condominium.
   b. cooperative.
   c. time share.
   d. town house.

51. The government exercises its power of eminent domain by the use of a court action called
   a. probate.
   b. laches.
   c. condemnation.
   d. certiorari.

52. If a property owner fails to pay taxes, the taxes can be collected by a legal process called
   a. adverse possession.
   b. condemnation.
   c. tax sale.
   d. dedication.

53. A house just sold for $250,000. The commission was paid as 7 percent of the sale price, 4 percent to the listing office and 3 percent to the selling office. What did the listing office receive?
   a. $17,000
   b. $7,500
   c. $12,000
   d. $10,000

54. A homeowner was taxed for curb and gutters. This tax is known as a
   a. general property tax.
   b. mechanic's lien.
   c. special assessment.
   d. prior appropriation.

55. The section due west of Section 1 within a township would be Section
   a. 2.
   b. 6.
   c. 12.
   d. 36.

56. An individual grantor can regulate land use by
   a. zoning restrictions.
   b. police power.
   c. deed restrictions.
   d. escheat.

57. A buyer thinks a price is too high because an equally desirable property can be purchased for less money. The buyer is practicing which principle?
   a. Highest and best use
   b. Anticipation
   c. Contribution
   d. Substitution

58. Four contiguous lots are valued at $10,000 each but if they were available as a single purchase they would be valued at $50,000 for the 4 lots. This is an example of
   a. progression.
   b. anticipation.
   c. competition.
   d. plottage.

59. Fee simple ownership of a dwelling unit plus a percentage ownership of common elements describes a
   a. condominium.
   b. cooperative.
   c. syndicate.
   d. general partnership.

60. Property that is held in severalty is owned by
   a. two or more persons in common.
   b. a single owner.
   c. a married couple.
   d. multiple owners with right of survivorship.

61. Albert has an permanent easement over Baker's adjoining property to get to his house. When Albert sells his house, the easment conveys to the new owner. This easement is
   a. servient.
   b. in gross.
   c. appurtenant.
   d. prescriptive.

62. The wall frame construction where one floor is built at a time using studs attached to upper and lower plates is known as
   a. platform frame construction.
   b. balloon frame construction.
   c. post-and-beam frame construction.
   d. pier and beam construction.

63. All four sides of a roof slope directly to the eaves. The roof style is known as a
   a. hip roof.
   b. gable roof.
   c. mansard roof.
   d. gambrel roof.

64. The New York Home Improvement Law applies to the sale of home improvement goods and services costing more than
    a. $50.
    b. $500.
    c. $5,000.
    d. $10,000.

65. Vertical wall framing members attached to a sill and spaced at regular intervals are known as
    a. headers.
    b. piers.
    c. studs.
    d. plates.

66. Which state agency regulates electrical systems and enforces the electrical code?
    a. HUD
    b. Board of Fire Underwriters
    c. DOS
    d. New York State Board of Electricity

67. Which of the following is NOT involved in regulating construction in New York?
    a. DOS
    b. DEP
    c. MTA
    d. EMF

68. When a local building code has stricter standards than the state code, which law prevails?
    a. The state code always prevails.
    b. The stricter standard prevails.
    c. Neither code applies because of the doctrine of inherent ambiguity.
    d. The builder can elect to build in accordance with either code.

69. The Civil Rights Act of 1866 prohibits discrimination based on
    a. race.
    b. race, color, religion, or national origin.
    c. handicaps and families with children.
    d. disabilities.

70. Before a building inspector can issue a Certificate of Occupancy, the inspector must make certain that
    a. mechanic liens have been satisfied.
    b. all required permits have been issued.
    c. the real estate agent involved is properly licensed.
    d. no back taxes are due.

71. A deed will not be accepted for recording unless it is accompanied by which of the following?
    a. A statement from the tax collector that all taxes have been paid.
    b. A Certificate of Occupancy
    c. A Real Property Transfer Report
    d. A copy of the abstract of title

72. When there is a gap in the chain of title, ownership can be established by a(n)
    a. partition action.
    b. condemnation proceeding.
    c. suit to quiet title.
    d. abstract.

73. A tenant in a mobile home park without a lease must be given how many days' notice of a rent increase?
    a. 30
    b. 60
    c. 90
    d. 180

74. A physically-disabled tenant wishes to remove door frames to provide the necessary width for a wheelchair. Based on these facts, which of the following statements is true?
    a. The tenant may not make any alterations.
    b. The tenant may be required to post a special repair bond to ensure that the premises will be restored at the end of the tenancy.
    c. The tenant may make the alteration, but must agree to restore the apartment to its original condition at the end of the tenancy.
    d. The landlord must make the alterations at his or her own expense.

75. Which of the following would be a credit to a buyer on a closing statement?
    a. Seller's commission payment
    b. Prepaid insurance
    c. Prepaid rents
    d. Sales price

76. The innocent landowner defense could not have been claimed prior to the enactment of
    a. SARA.
    b. CERCLA.
    c. Title VII.
    d. RESPA.

77. A broker who finds a ready, willing, and able buyer for a property is referred to as the
    a. special agent.
    b. procuring cause.
    c. fiduciary.
    d. dual agent.

78. Statements of opinion that exaggerate a property's benefits are called
    a. puffing.   c. fraud.
    b. latent defects.   d. ratification.

79. All of the following are characteristics of a ready, willing and able buyer, *EXCEPT*
    a. prepared to buy on the seller's terms.
    b. willing to pay the full commission.
    c. prepared to conclude the transaction.
    d. financially capable.

80. The broker with whom a seller enters into a valid listing agreement is the
    a. listing agent.   c. selling broker.
    b. cooperating broker.   d. exclusive agent.

81. A listing agreement in which the broker's compensation is the amount above the seller's required proceeds is a(n)
    a. legal dual agency.
    b. illegal subagency.
    a. illegal net listing.
    b. legal net listing.

82. From the broker's standpoint, the most desirable type of listing is an
    a. exclusive-agency listing.
    b. exclusive-right-to-sell listing.
    c. open listing.
    d. implied subagency listing.

83. An agreement among members of a trade to exclude other members from fair participation is
    a. price-fixing.   c. a tie-in.
    b. group boycotting.   d. allocation.

84. An MLS may legally engage in which of the following activities?
    a. Restrict members' business activities
    b. Deny reasonable access to its services
    c. Restrict the properties members may list
    d. Impose membership requirements and fees

85. All of the following are economic character-istics of land, *EXCEPT*
    a. indestructibility.   c. improvements.
    b. scarcity.   d. area preference.

86. A property's market value is
    a. an estimate of how much it would cost to rebuild the structure, less depreciation.
    b. a measurement of the worth of a property based on its income-producing capacity.
    c. the same as the asking price.
    d. the price it will command in a free and open market, in a voluntary, arm's length transaction.

87. A written statement sworn to before an authorized officer of the court is a(n)
    a. novation.   c. proration.
    b. caveat.   d. affidavit.

88. The standard package homeowner's insurance policy coverage for personal injuries to others as a result of the insured's acts of negligence is
    a. liability coverage.
    b. replacement coverage.
    c. coinsurance coverage.
    d. hazard insurance coverage.

89. The percentage a borrower is required to pay above the mortgage index is referred to as the
    a. adjustor.   c. ceiling.
    b. PMI.   d. margin.

90. Which of the following regulates real estate advertisements that refer to mortgage terms?
    a. ECOA   c. FHLMC
    b. Regulation Z d. RESPA

91. The 3-day right of rescission under Regulation Z applies to which of the following transactions?
   a. Residential purchase-money first-mortgages
   b. Refinanced loans
   c. Commercial loans
   d. Business loans

92. The Equal Credit Opportunity Act prohibits discrimination in lending and credit transactions on the basis of all the following, EXCEPT
   a. race.
   b. income.
   c. marital status.
   d. welfare.

93. Curb appeal refers to which of the following?
   a. A building's overall exterior appearance
   b. The condition of the street in front of the property
   c. A yard sign or other display
   d. Neighboring properties' market values

94. What is the limit on late rent payment charges for mobile home tenants, after a 10-day grace period has expired?
   a. $100
   b. 1 month's rent
   c. 5 percent
   d. one

95. If a landlord wants to change the rules of a mobile home park, how many days must he or she wait after giving tenants written notice?
   a. 30
   b. 60
   c. 90
   d. None

96. Foyers, hallways, and landscaping are examples of
   a. personal property.
   b. conversion elements.
   c. common elements.
   d. nonconforming uses.

97. What is a unit owner's evidence of an ownership interest in a cooperative property?
   a. Proprietary lease
   b. Bylaws
   c. Overlying mortgage
   d. Assessment certificate

98. Uniformity of tax assessment among districts that assess at different rates may be achieved by
   a. full-value assessment.
   b. an equalization factor.
   c. appropriation.
   d. applying exemptions.

99. The maximum range of rate adjustment permitted over the life of an adjustable-rate loan is the
   a. cap.
   b. ceiling.
   c. margin.
   d. annuity.

100. An individual who is authorized to represent the principal in all matters that can possibly be delegated is referred to as a(n)
   a. fiduciary agent.
   b. special agent.
   c. general agent.
   d. universal agent.

BROKER'S PRACTICE EXAM II

1. All of the following are factors that may be used to distinguish an employee from an independent contractor in a real estate office, *EXCEPT*
   a. manner of compensation.
   b. degree of control.
   c. licensed or unlicensed.
   d. written agreement.

2. How many additional hours of study are required for a licensed salesperson to become a broker in New York?
   a. 10
   b. 25
   c. 0
   d. 45

3. All of the following would be considered fraudulent acts, *EXCEPT*
   a. a broker chooses not to disclose certain unpleasant but important facts about a property.
   b. a broker tells a prospective buyer certain facts about a proprety that the broker knows are untrue.
   c. a broker decides not to tell a buyer who is about to make an offer on a house that the neighboring property has been rezoned for heavy industrial use.
   d. a broker unintentionally misinforms a buyer by passing on information supplied by the owner.

4. Which of the following is a form of co-ownership that passes automatically to the surviving co-owners when one of the co-owners dies?
   a. Tenancy-in-common
   b. Joint tenancy
   c. Corporate ownership
   d. Syndicate ownership

5. In an adjustable-rate mortgage, the interest rate is raised or lowered depending on the behavior of a particular
   a. mortgage-backed security.
   b. mortgage rate index.
   c. amortization table.
   d. underwriter.

6. Representing both principal parties in the same transaction, without full written disclosure of the fact and the parties' consent, is referred to as
   a. undisclosed dual agency.
   b. undisclosed subagency.
   c. subagency-by-ratification.
   d. implied agency.

7. Which of the following correctly expresses the difference between an employee and an independent contractor?
   a. Employers have greater day-to-day control over the work of an independent contractor.
   b. Independent contractors are more likely than employees to participate in employer-funded health care and pension plans.
   c. Brokers are not required to withhold taxes from payments made to independent contractors.
   d. Independent contractors are usually compensated on an hourly basis, rather than simply for performance.

8. For how many years must an individual have open, notorious, continuous, uninterrupted, exclusive and adverse use of another's property to acquire an easement by prescription in New York?
   a. 7
   b. 10
   c. 15
   d. 25

9. All of the following are government actors in the secondary mortgage market, *EXCEPT*
   a. FNMA.
   b. HUD.
   c. FHLMC.
   d. GNMA.

10. A broker formed a real estate business as a sole proprietorship. All of the following are true of the new business, *EXCEPT*
   a. the broker is entitled to take profits as income.
   b. the broker's salary is subject to dual taxation.
   c. the tax advantages of the sole proprietorship form are well-suited to a small business.
   d. the broker's financial liability is unlimited.

11. On a closing statement, items of expense that have been incurred, but are not yet payable, are referred to as
   a. incurred items.
   b. accrued items.
   c. liabilities.
   d. prepaid items.

12. In New York, the right of election is available to
   a. a surviving spouse only.
   b. the statutory heirs of a decedent.
   c. any surviving relative who gives notice within 30 days of the opening of probate.
   d. the decedent's children only.

13. A pro forma is a
   a. report of property's actual past income-generating performance.
   b. measurement of the degree of investor involvement.
   c. projection of a property's likely performance in the future.
   d. device for calculating the effect of leveraging on accelerated depreciation.

14. A lease that automatically renews for similar succeeding periods creates what type of tenancy?
   a. At will
   b. Periodic
   c. At sufferance
   d. For years

15. Homes that are produced in a factory and then trucked to a prepared building site to be set onto a foundation are referred to what type of homes?
   a. Prebuilt
   b. Panelized
   c. Modular
   d. Permanent mobile

16. When the parties to a transaction agree on the essential terms, what is said to have taken place?
   a. A procuring cause of sale
   b. Ratification
   c. Meeting of the minds
   d. Self-dealing

17. The Sherman Act and the Clayton Act are examples of
   a. federal fair employment laws.
   b. New York State vicarious liability laws.
   c. federal antitrust laws.
   d. Workers' compensation laws.

18. Jones built a garage that was mostly on his property. The northwest corner, however, lay three feet over the property line onto Vell's property. Which of the following best describes this situation?
   a. Easement in gross
   b. Involuntary lien
   c. Encroachment
   d. Easement appurtenant

19. Are a salesperson and a broker allowed to form a real estate office partnership in New York?
   a. Yes, as long as both hold currently active licenses.
   b. Yes, if they both hold equal interests.
   c. Yes, if they register as employee and principal, respectively.
   d. No.

20. A group of local real estate brokers agree to form an open membership organization to share their listings with one another. Based on these facts alone, is this activity legal?
  a. No, it is an illegal allocation of a market
  b. No, it constitutes an illegal restraint of trade.
  c. No, it is essentially illegal price-fixing.
  d. Yes, it is essentially a multiple-listing service.

21. A real estate broker is usually which type of agent?
  a. Special   **c.** Universal
  b. General   **d.** Gratuitous

22. The Federal Fair Housing Act prohibits discrimination in the sale or rental of residential housing on the basis of all the following, *EXCEPT*
  a. income from public assistance.
  b. race or color.
  c. familial status.
  d. nation of origin.

23. In the rectangular survey system, townships are divided into 36 sections of how many acres each?
  a. 1   **c.** 360
  b. 240   **d.** 640

24. In an adjustable-rate mortgage, the limitation on the size of any single adjustment during the life of the loan is referred to as a(n)
  a. ceiling.   **c.** margin.
  b. index.   **d.** cap.

25. The net spendable income generated by an investment is referred to as
  a. capital gain.   **c.** cash flow.
  b. depreciation.   **d.** leverage.

26. An agent who mixes his or her clients' funds with his or her own personal funds is engaging in
  a. collateral estoppel.
  b. escrow.
  c. commingling.
  d. misrepresentation.

27. An agent who is empowered to represent the principal in a specific range of matters, and who may bind the principal to any contract within the scope of the agent's authority is what kind of agent?
  a. Universal   **c.** General
  b. Special   **d.** Procuring

28. All of the following are fiduciary duties owed by an agent to a principal, *EXCEPT*
  a. loyalty.   **c.** obedience.
  b. accounting.   **d.** interest.

29. A mortgage that exceeds the maximum limits set by FNMA and FHLMC is what kind of loan?
  a. Jumbo   **c.** Off-index
  b. Convertible   **d.** Premium

30. To become a real estate broker in New York, an individual must have how many months of experience as a salesperson?
  a. 6   **c.** 18
  b. 12   **d.** 24

31. Under New York law, which of the following are required to fully disclose the nature and extent of their agency relationships to any party with whom they have substantive contact?
  a. Brokers only
  b. Brokers and salespersons
  c. Sellers only
  d. Buyers, sellers and brokers, but not salespersons

32. All of the following leases are enforceable in New York, *EXCEPT*
  a. a written lease for 15 months.
  b. an oral lease for 6 months.
  c. an oral lease for 23 months.
  d. an acknowledged, recorded 3-year lease.

33. A person who is in the business of bringing people together, for a fee or commission, for the purpose of buying, selling, exchanging or leasing real estate, is referred to as a(n)
  a. agent.   **c.** fiduciary.
  b. broker.   **d.** principal.

34. An amount entered on a closing statement in a person's favor, that has been paid or which must be reimbursed, is a(n)
    a. debit.
    b. accrued item.
    c. credit.
    d. caveat.

35. In a life estate, who has a present right to the property if the estate holder dies while the measuring life is still alive?
    a. The measuring life
    b. The estate holder's heirs
    c. The measuring life's heirs
    d. The grantor's heirs

36. Caveat Emptor means
    a. seller beware.
    b. broker beware.
    c. buyer beware.
    d. client beware.

37. Voluntary medical payments for injuries sustained by guests or resident employees on the insured property are covered by what insurance?
    a. Hazard
    b. Liability
    c. Lender's
    d. Local property

38. Which type of deed provides the most protection for grantees?
    a. Bargain and sale
    b. Quitclaim
    c. Covenant
    d. General warranty

39. Title that is good or clear, and reasonably free from the risk of lawsuits over defects, is
    a. viable.
    b. marketable.
    c. constructive.
    d. ctual.

40. Which of the following types of leases usually involves a long-term lease of land only?
    a. Net lease
    b. Gross lease
    c. Ground lease
    d. Percentage lease

41. A broker may compel his independent contractor to
    a. attend office meetings.
    b. earn a specific amount of commissions.
    c. comply with office policy and DOS regulations.
    d. work a specific work week.

42. A mortgage in which the interest rate is raised or lowered during specific periods to reflect the behavior of an index is what type of mortgage?
    a. Conventional
    b. Indexed
    c. Fixed-rate
    d. Adjustable-rate

43. A broker is required to
    a. monitor, train, and supervise the agents under him.
    b. pay for his agents' continuing education.
    c. require his agents to purchase E&O insurance to relieve him from agent responsibility.
    d. report all infractions to DOS.

44. A legal proceeding to divide a property that is jointly owned by two or more parties, when the cotenants cannot agree on the use or disposition of the property, is called
    a. adverse possession.
    b. tacking.
    c. partition.
    d. action to quiet title.

45. A contract in which some term or condition remains to be performed or fulfilled is what type of contract?
    a. Executed
    b. Invalid
    c. Unilateral
    d. Executory

46. The broker who successfully finds a ready, willing and able buyer for a property is referred to as the
    a. listing broker.
    b. selling broker.
    c. agent.
    d. subagent.

47. Collection and analysis of suspect materials on or near a property is characteristic of which phase of an environmental audit?
    a. I
    b. II
    c. III
    d. IV

48. The party who receives property by will is known as the
a. devisee.
b. testatee.
c. bequestor.
d. grantee.

49. If a foreclosure sale fails to generate sufficient funds to pay off the mortgage debt, the mortgagee may seek what kind of judgment?
a. Deficiency
b. Equity
c. Satisfaction
d. Alienation

50. In New York, a surviving spouse is always entitled to the greater of $50,000 plus what portion of the remainder of the estate?
a. One-quarter
b. One-half
c. One-third
d. Two-thirds

51. Cash flow + mortgage amortization + appreciation + tax benefits =
a. net operating income
b. total return on investment
c. operating expenses
d. gross expense of investment

52. A charge levied against a development to help the surrounding community deal with the additional demands for services, utilities and schools is a(n)
a. population adjustment fee (PAF).
b. impact fee.
c. special assessment levy.
d. service maintenance charge (SMC).

53. One point is the equivalent of
a. 1/100th of the sales price.
b. 1 percent of the loan amount.
c. 10 percent of the loan amount.
d. one monthly payment, including principal, interest, taxes, and insurance.

54. Ownership of which of the following is evidenced by a proprietary lease?
a. Condominium
b. Cooperative
c. Time-share
d. Rent-controlled apartment

55. The amount added to an adjustable-rate mortgage's interest rate to cover the lender's costs is called the
a. boot.
b. margin.
c. cap.
d. index.

56. What type of prefabricated housing is assembled on-site from segments, such as roof trusses and walls, that are produced elsewhere and shipped to the lot?
a. Panelized housing
b. Modular homes
c. Assembly-homes
d. Part-built homes

57. Substituting a new contract or parties in place of the original is referred to as
a. release.
b. novation.
c. assignment.
d. implication.

58. Tenants in a mobile home park must be offered leases of at least how long?
a. 1 month
b. 6 months
c. 1 year
d. 18 months

59. A loan in which the principal and interest is payable in monthly installments over the whole term is what type of loan?
a. ARM
b. Straight
c. Amortized
d. Accelerated

60. What is the purpose of the real estate license law?
a. To provide the GRI designation to qualified candidates
b. To certify real estate agents.
c. To protect the public from fraud and set standards of professionalism
d. To restrict the free operation of legitimate real estate enterprises in the state of New York

61. The reversion of property to the state or county when a landowner dies intestate and without heirs, is
a. escheat.
b. laches.
c. condemnation.
d. certiorari.

62. Certain disclosures to purchasers of residential property about settlement costs are required by
   a. HUD.
   b. the Torrens System.
   c. FHA.
   d. RESPA.

63. The party who makes a will is known as the
   a. devisee.
   b. testator.
   c. legatee.
   d. grantor.

64. Gross rental income minus expenses yields
   a. cash flow.
   b. net operating income.
   c. total return on investment.
   d. depreciation.

65. An owner who feels his property taxes are too high may
   a. file a tax grievance with the municipality.
   b. refuse to pay it.
   c. take his case to small claims court.
   d. complain to the building department.

66. The construction of a two-bedroom ranch-style brick home in a neighborhood of ranch-style brick homes would comply with the principle of
   a. substitution.
   b. competition.
   c. conformity.
   d. anticipation.

67. Compensation in the form of an agreed-upon percentage of the selling price of a property is called a(n)
   a. listing.
   b. market value.
   c. commission.
   d. kickback.

68. A seller is free to employ as many brokers as he or she wishes, and must pay a commission only to the broker who successfully produces a qualified buyer in what type of listing?
   a. Net
   b. Exclusive-right-to-sell
   c. Open
   d. Unlimited

69. The standard residential electrical circuit, composed of one hot and one neutral wire, and a separate ground wire, is
   a. 60 watt.
   b. 100-volt.
   c. 110-volt
   d. 220-volt.

70. What kind of agent is a property manager, under most management agreements?
   a. Special
   b. General
   c. Limited
   d. Operational

71. A certificate of title and a Torrens certificate are both
   a. chain of title items.
   b. evidence of title insurance.
   c. evidence of title.
   d. evidence of acutal notice.

72. A recorded deed restriction may be enforced by a violator's neighbors by a lawsuit seeking
   a. laches.
   b. an injunction.
   c. a zoning ordinance.
   d. a declaration of restrictions.

73. A municipality can control development, population density and building heights through
   a. escheat.
   b. zoning.
   c. laches.
   d. deed restrictions

74. Rent control regulations apply to buildings with how many units, if built before 1947 and continuously occupied by the current tenant since July 1, 1971?
   a. Two or more
   b. Three or more
   c. Five or fewer
   d. Any number

75. The federal law that prohibits discrimination against credit applicants on the basis of race, color, religion, national origin and other factors is
   a. RESPA.
   b. ECOA.
   c. CERCLA.
   d. Regulation Z.

76. A real estate broker whose office engages in restraint of trade is violating the
   a. Civil Rights Act of 1868.
   b. Sherman Anti-trust Act.
   c. General Obligations Law.
   d. Law of Agency.

77. In New York, what is the statute of limitations on the right of neighboring owners to object to violations of the general plan of a subdivision?
   a. One year
   b. Two years
   c. Seven years
   d. Ten years

78. The income capitalization approach measures the value of a property based on
   a. the amount of income it generates over time.
   b. the estimated cost to rebuild the structure, minus depreciation.
   c. the price the property would command in an open market, in a free, arm's length transaction between informed, willing parties.
   d. the alternative uses to which the prospective buyer's funds could be put to generate a profit.

79. The difference between the present value of all positive and negative cash flows is referred to as
   a. NPV.   c. NOI
   b. IRR   d. GRI

80. A report of recent sales of similar properties, intended to assist an owner in setting a reasonable listing price based on current market factors is a(n)
   a. appraisal.
   b. present value summary (PVS).
   c. comparative market analysis (CMA).
   d. current market abstract (CMA).

81. With regard to VA loans made after March 1, 1988
   a. the assumptor must be a veteran.
   b. the assumptor does not have to meet any special financial qualification requirements, but must be a veteran.
   c. the assumptor need not be a veteran, but must prove creditworthiness.
   d. such loans are non-assumable.

82. All of the following constitute discriminatory actions on the part of the broker, *EXCEPT*
   a. refusing to deal with an individual because of his or her race.
   b. telling a prospective tenant that there are no units available in an apartment building, when in fact units are available.
   c. offering complete relocation services to Roman Catholics, while Protestants are left to leaf through the MLS book unassisted.
   d. showing properties to prospective buyers only in certain, specific neighborhoods the buyers ask to see.

83. Local taxing bodies may offer partial exemptions from property taxes on primary residences owned by individuals who are
   a. 55 years of age or older, without regard to income.
   b. 65 years of age or older, with modest incomes.
   c. at least 62 years old, regardless of income.
   d. at least 74 years old, with modest incomes.

84. A roofing system that relies on sloping timbers supported by a ridge board and made rigid by interconnecting joists is what kind of roof?
   a. Truss   c. Exposed rafter
   b. Joist and rafter   d. Gable

85. Impaired physical and mental development in children is a symptom of which of the following environmental hazards?
   a. Inhaling asbestos fibers
   b. Presence of leaking underground storage tanks
   c. Lead poisoning
   d. Radon gas exposure

86. Asbestos must always
   a. be removed.
   b. encapsulated.
   c. be remediated according to the specific problem, if it all.
   d. left alone.

87. A loss of value due to poor design or age of a property is what type of obsolescence?
   a. Functional   c. Physical
   b. External   d. Interior

88. Evidence that a construction project has satisfied the minimum standards of the local building department is provided by a
   a. Certificate of Minimum Standards.
   b. Certificate of Occupancy.
   c. Building permit.
   d. License to Occupy.

89. The terms of each tenant's lease, the quantity of rentable space and the overall quality and physical condition of the property are elements of what kind of analysis?
    a. Neighborhood
    b. Regional
    c. Market
    d. Property

90. Laws designed to prevent employers from making their hiring and firing decisions on factors unrelated to job performance are referred to as
    a. antitrust laws.
    b. guaranteed employment laws.
    c. anti-firing laws.
    d. fair employment laws.

91. Throughout New York State, landlords of buildings with three or more apartments must provide tenants with all the following, EXCEPT
    a. smoke detectors.
    b. vermin-free premises.
    c. information about lead-based paint.
    d. functioning air conditioning systems.

92. A surrogate court proceeding to rule on the validity of a will, the identity of the devisees and the portions of the estate due to each party is
    a. involuntary alienation.
    b. condemnation.
    c. probate.
    d. escheat.

93. If unmortgaged vacant property is sold by the county to satisfy a delinquent tax lien, the defaulted owner is entitled to redeem the property within how long after the date of the tax sale?
    a. Six months
    b. One year
    c. Two years
    d. There is no such right of redemtion after a tax sale is held.

94. The principle that the worth of a lesser-quality property is enhanced by the presence of a nearby property of greater quality is
    a. proximity.
    b. progression.
    c. competition.
    d. enhancement.

95. Which of the following agency relationships, if entered into without a full written disclosure and consent of the parties, is illegal in New York?
    a. Open
    b. Dual
    c. Seller
    d. Cooperative

96. A loan that is paid in 26 half-month payments each year is referred to as what type of mortgage?
    a. Amortized
    b. Biweekly
    c. Balloon
    d. Bimonthly

97. A person who dies without making a will is said to be
    a. in probate.
    b. intestate.
    c. a testate.
    d. a nonlegator.

98. The principle that no physical or economic condition remains constant is
    a. progression.
    b. change.
    c. flux.
    d. anticipation.

99. A short-term loan designed to cover a gap between the sale of one property and the purchase of another is known as a(n)
    a. bullet loan.
    b. jumbo loan.
    c. margin loan.
    d. bridge loan

100. Remediation occurs in which phase of an environmental audit?
    a. I
    b. II
    c. III
    d. Remediation is not part of the environmental auditing process.

ANSWER KEY FOR
BROKER'S PRACTICE EXAMS

With Chapter references to *Modern Real Estate Practice in New York*, 8th Edition.

PRACTICE EXAM I

1. b 1
2. b 1
3. a 1
4. c 3
5. c 12
6. d 16
7. c 1
8. b 11
9. a 3
10. c 3
11. b 3
12. d 3
13. d 19
14. a 19
15. d 16
16. d 9
17. c 1
18. b 2
19. d 12
20. a 20
21. b 11
22. d 10
23. b 10
24. b 11
25. a 12
26. d 10
27. c 10
28. a 21
29. d 21
30. c 5
31. c 5
32. a 21
33. c 8
34. d 7
35. b 8
36. b 7
37. c 25
38. b 25
39. a 6
40. d 8
41. a 24
42. b 24
43. c 8

44. d 24
45. b 24
46. a 23
47. c 23
48. d 23
49. b 23
50. b 23
51. c 12
52. c 26
53. d 26
54. c 26
55. a 6
56. c 12
57. d 14
58. d 14
59. a 4
60. b 4
61. c 5
62. a 13
63. a 13
64. b 13
65. c 13
66. b 23
67. d 23
68. b 23
69. a 15
70. b 23
71. c 9
72. c 9
73. c 25
74. c 15
75. c 9
76. a 16
77. b 2
78. a 2
79. b 2
80. a 3
81. c 3
82. b 3
83. b 19
84. d 19
85. a 14
86. d 14
87. d 9

88. a 9
89. d 11
90. b 11
91. b 11
92. b 11
93. a 25
94. c 25
95. a 25
96. c 23
97. a 23
98. b 26
99. b 11
100. d 2

PRACTICE EXAM II

1. c 18
2. d 1
3. d 2
4. b 4
5. b 11
6. a 3
7. c 18
8. b 5
9. b 20
10. b 19
11. b 9
12. a 24
13. c 21
14. b 7
15. c 23
16. c 2
17. c 19
18. c 5
19. d 1
20. d 19
21. a 2
22. a 15
23. d 6
24. d 11
25. c 21
26. c 1
27. c 2
28. d 2
29. a 11

30.	b	1	54.	b	23	78.	a	14
31.	b	3	55.	b	11	79.	a	21
32.	c	7	56.	a	23	80.	c	14
33.	b	2	57.	b	8	81.	c	11
34.	c	9	58.	c	25	82.	d	15
35.	b	4	59.	c	10	83.	b	26
36.	c	23	60.	c	1	84.	b	13
37.	b	9	61.	a	12	85.	c	16
38.	d	6	62.	d	9	86.	c	16
39.	b	9	63.	b	24	87.	a	14
40.	c	7	64.	b	21	88.	b	23
41.	c	18	65.	a	26	89.	d	25
42.	d	10	66.	c	14	90.	d	19
43.	a	2	67.	c	2	91.	d	25
44.	c	24	68.	c	3	92.	c	24
45.	d	8	69.	c	13	93.	b	26
46.	b	3	70.	b	25	94.	b	14
47.	b	23	71.	c	9	95.	b	3
48.	a	24	72.	b	23	96.	b	10
49.	a	10	73.	b	12	97.	b	24
50.	c	24	74.	b	25	98.	b	14
51.	b	21	75.	b	11	99.	d	11
52.	b	23	76.	b	19	100.	c	23
53.	b	10	77.	b	23			